EROTIC VERSE

EROTIC VERSE

EDITED BY

Christopher Hurford

Robinson
London

Robinson Publishing Ltd
7 Kensington Church Court
London w8 4sp

First published in Great Britain by Robinson Publishing Ltd 1995

A copy of the British Library Cataloguing in Publication Data
is available from the British Library

ISBN 1–85487–396–2

Printed and bound in the EC

10 9 8 7 6 5 4 3 2 1

CONTENTS

Introduction   **xi**

ATTRACTION

Delight in disorder   *Robert Herrick*   3
Wasted days   *Oscar Wilde*   4
The ninth secret poem   *Guillaume Apollinaire*   5
Upon a mole in Celia's bosom   *Thomas Carew*   6
The compliment   *Thomas Carew*   7

SEDUCTION

from The Song of Solomon   13
Ballata concerning a shepherd-maid   *Guido Cavalcanti*   15
To Amasia, tickling a gentleman   *John Hopkins*   16
The geranium   *Richard Brinsley Sheridan*   17
Be quiet, Sir!   *Anon*   19
Sylvia the fair   *John Dryden*   20
A lover out of fashion   *Sir John Davies*   21
A young violinist from Rio   *Anon*   22

THE DEED

from Don Juan, Canto II   *George Gordon, Lord Byron*   25
may i feel said he   *e. e. cummings*   27
Sonnet LXIV   *Edmund Spenser*   29
Clothes do but cheat and cozen us   *Robert Herrick*   30
The platonic blow   *W. H. Auden*   31
To his mistress going to bed   *John Donne*   33
from The delights of Venus   *Meursius*   35
Amynta led me to a grove   *Aphra Behn*   39

Doing, a filthy pleasure is, and short   *Petronius*   40
On fruition   *Sir Charles Sedley*   41
To his coy mistress   *Andrew Marvell*   42
Dainty darling   *Anon*   44
from Metamorphoses, Book IV   *Ovid*   45
from De rerum natura, Book IV   *Lucretius*   47
Corydon and Phyllis   *Sir Charles Sedley*   48
Blessed as the immortal gods   *Sappho*   50
As I was walking   *Anon*   51
In days of old when knights were bold   *Anon*   51
According to old Sigmund Freud   *Anon*   52
There was a young plumber of Leigh   *Arnold Bennett* (attr.)   52

A BIT OF THE OTHER

Something of a departure   *Paul Muldoon*   55
from The Delights of Venus   *Meursius*   56
To a plum-coloured bra displayed in Marks & Spencer
   Gavin Ewart   57
Song   *John Wilmot, Earl of Rochester*   58
Gellius is thin   *Catullus*   60
In Francum   *Sir John Davies*   60
Kisses loathsome   *Robert Herrick*   61
from Christabel   *Samuel Taylor Coleridge*   62
Each man his humour hath   *Sir John Suckling*   63
from Goblin market   *Christina Rossetti*   64
Gellius, why are your lips   *Catullus*   65
An epitaph   *Anon*   65
Seymour and Chantelle or Un peu de vice   *Stevie Smith*   66
from Dildoides   *Samuel Butler*   68
from Charmides   *Oscar Wilde*   72
from Don Leon   *Anon*   75
There was a young student of Johns   *Anon*   76
There was a young fellow of Lyme   *Anon*   76
The new cinematic emporium   *Anon*   77
A weakling who lacked protoplasm   *Anon*   77
A fellow with passions quite gingery   *Anon*   78
A short-sighted sailor from Brighton   *Anon*   78
A gay boy who lived in Khartoum   *Anon*   79
There was a young couple called Kelly   *Anon*   79

LOVE AND LUST

Cleft for me   *Gavin Ewart*   83
In summer's heat   *Ovid*   84
An ever-fixed mark   *Kingsley Amis*   85
from De rerum natura, Book IV   *Lucretius*   86
i like my body when it is with your   *e. e. cummings*   88
A woman waits for me   *Walt Whitman*   89
Love and sleep   *Algernon Charles Swinburne*   91
Ipsithilla, baby girl   *Catullus*   92
from Satires VI   *Juvenal*   93
Circe   *Gavin Ewart*   94
from I sing the body electric   *Walt Whitman*   95
Between your sheets   *Lady Mary Wortley Montagu*   96
The feel of hands   *Thom Gunn*   97
from Venus and Adonis   *William Shakespeare*   98
A letter from the Lord Buckhurst to Mr George Etherege
    Charles Sackville, Lord Buckhurst   101
from Don Leon   *Anon*   103
'Given faith', sighed the vicar of Deneham   *Anon*   104
There was a young lady of Dover   *Anon*   104
There was a young fellow of King's   *Anon*   105
A wanton young lady of Wimley   *Anon*   105
Amen   *Anon*   106

FAST AND LOOSE

Sodom, a satyr on Charles II   *John Wilmot, Earl of*
    Rochester   109
Low scene   *Paul Verlaine*   110
from The priapean corpus, XXVI   *Anon*   111
Against an old lecher   *Sir John Harington*   112
Elegies, Book I   *Ovid*   113
Hye nonny nonny noe   *Anon*   115
The denial   *Anon*   117
A drinker and a wencher   *Anon*   118
Régime de vivre   *John Wilmot, Earl of Rochester*   119
Of an heroical answer of a great Roman lady to her husband
    Sir John Harington   120
A ramble in St James's Park   *John Wilmot, Earl of Rochester* 121

Nell Gwynne   *Anon*   126
Molly   *Anon*   127
A modern young woman from France   *Anon*   127

BELL ENDS AND BEAVERS

Figs   *D. H. Lawrence*   131
The author to his wife, of a woman's eloquence
   Sir John Harington   134
Um Chukka Willy   *Anon*   135
I have a noble cockerel   *Anon*   136
Epigram XXXIII   *Martial*   137
A beehive   *Anon*   137
One writing against his prick   *Anon*   138
Upon the nipples of Julia's breast   *Robert Herrick*   139
Epigrams on Priapus   *Anon*   140
from The priapean corpus, IX   *Anon*   141
The tenement   *Anon*   142
Epigram XXXIV   *Martial*   144
Terminology   *Anon*   145
A riddle   *Anon*   146
Nine inch will please a lady   *Robert Burns*   147
In winter, in my room   *Emily Dickinson*   148
Stand, stately Tavie   *Anon*   150
The hairy prospect   *Thomas Rowlandson* (attr.)   150
Busts and bosoms have I known   *Anon*   151
My friend Billy   *Anon*   151
There was a young man of Devizes   *Anon*   152
There once was a young man of Ghent   *Anon*   152

DAMP SQUIBS AND OTHER DISAPPOINTMENTS

On a bashful shepherd   *'Ephelia'*   155
To his mistress, objecting to him neither toying nor talking
   Robert Herrick   156
She lay all naked   *Anon*   157
The imperfect enjoyment   *John Wilmot, Earl of Rochester*   159
The sick rose   *William Blake*   161
Walking in a meadow green   *Anon*   162
The women's complaint to Venus   *Anon*   164

I, being born a woman and distressed   *Edna St Vincent*
    Millay   165
The vine   *Robert Herrick*   166
Elegies, III   *Ovid*   167
from The disappointment   *Aphra Behn*   169
Here lies the body   *Anon*   172
There was a young actress called Sue   *Anon*   173
A lonely young man from Norway   *Anon*   173
A remarkable tribe are the Sweenies   *Anon*   174
There was a young man from Berlin   *Anon*   174
An unfortunate pirate called Bates   *Anon*   175
A beautiful lass from Saigon   *Anon*   175

YEARNING

from Carmina Burana   *Anon*   179
The vision   *Robert Herrick*   180
In a gondola   *Robert Browning*   181
Faded leaves: Longing   *Matthew Arnold*   182
Echo   *Christina Rossetti*   183
The Eve of St Agnes   *John Keats*   184
Celia   *Matthew Prior*   196

FROM THE CRADLE TO THE GRAVE

Fat Molly   *Paul Durcan*   199
To a Sicilian boy   *Theodore Wratislaw*   201
Song   *John Wilmot, Earl of Rochester*   202
Late-flowering lust   *John Betjeman*   203
The second rapture   *Thomas Carew*   204
Friendship   *Katherine Mansfield*   205
A song of a young lady to her ancient lover   *John Wilmot,*
    Earl of Rochester   206
Epigram XXIX   *Martial*   207
from Hero and Leander   *Christopher Marlowe*   208
from Goblin market   *Christina Rossetti*   210
The days of my youth   *Anon*   211
Epigram   *Anon*   212
Gather ye rosebuds   *Anon*   213
An old prostitute from Marseilles   *Anon*   213

A candle *Sir John Suckling*   217
Upon the author of the play called *Sodom* *John Oldham*   218
Epitaph for Oscar Wilde *Charles Algernon Swinburne*   220
Lady H— to Mrs P— *Anon*   221
The harlot of Jerusalem *Anon*   222
O'Reilly's daughter *Anon*   226
Eskimo Nell *Anon*   228
Nine times a night *Anon*   234
In Mobile *Anon*   235
Gay Furius, Aurelius *Catullus*   239
from The Prologue to The Wife of Bath's Tale
  Geoffrey Chaucer   240
The good ship *Venus* *Anon*   245
There was a young girl whose frigidity *Anon*   250
There was a young woman from Harlesden *Anon*   250
In the Garden of Eden lay Adam *Anon*   251

Index of first lines   253
Acknowledgements   258

INTRODUCTION

In the late twentieth century there can be little doubt that sex has become a popular subject. Although people have always thought about it more often (and have done it less frequently) than they care to admit, sex has recently found a very prominent place in popular magazines, chat shows, films – everywhere, in fact – except for poetry.

The whole subject of sexual verse – and I mean an upfront, unabashed, witty celebration of sex – has either become an obscure specialist field for highbrow collectors, or a collection of unrepeatable ditties handed down by word of mouth from generation to generation of rugby players. On the one hand there are whispered rumours in libraries about infamous versifiers such as Rochester or Rimbaud, and on the other, those cheap books of limericks that Auntie furtively gives Dad for Christmas, which no one ever sees again.

Which is a shame, because we have a wealth of erotic, bawdy and generally steamy poetry simmering away beneath the surface of good taste. The fact that it is either hushed up or poo-pooed is no doubt due to centuries of squeamishness, and that curious fear that poetry (of all things) corrupts minds both old and young. Which is why those cheap Christmas anthologies seem just to disappear. I can clearly remember as a child finding one of Auntie's presents to Dad stowed away, unread but out of reach, at the back of the wardrobe. It was harmless stuff, but it was the nearest I'd yet come to knowing what sex was all about. And reading it felt like committing a major sin, which of course was wonderful.

While truly great sexual poetry can generate such feelings of frisky devilishness even in the most ancient of readers, let us hope it can be read these days a little more openly, and with less embarrassment. Even wicked verses by great writers have been hushed up and rarely printed, which makes these literary giants seem a lot stuffier than they actually were. Auden, for example, wrote some very graphic verses for his friends, while boring old Romans such as Ovid and Catullus produced a number of sizzlers. Even publishers have felt restrained, and as late as 1953 decided not to publish Rochester's 'The imperfect enjoyment' (page 159) for fear of offending against Britain's obscenity laws.

Guardians of Literature never did know how to cope with sex, which is why they generally sniff at that most prolific and popular author, Anon. This poet has been penning humorous, scandalous and blue verse for centuries, and his or her favourite type of poetry is the limerick. The great advantage of this poetic form is that, like Anon, it has never been taken seriously. This means it can joke about anything it wants, from the most extraordinary sexual positions to gigantic organs and the joys of venereal warts. And repeating a limerick also means that you can joke about sex under the cover of poetry. My grandmother, who is usually a sober kind of lady, knows hundreds of the very dirtiest limericks, and she delights in reciting them to her eternally surprised doctor. Several of her favourites are included here.

This anthology, then, is a shameless celebration of all types of sexual poetry, with less of the boudoir and more of the bedroom. As it is meant for browsing, I have divided the book into the kinds of subjects which may be uppermost in an enquiring reader's mind – such as seduction itself, bodily parts, curious perversions and poems about actually doing it. The chapter titles speak for themselves, I hope. Needless to say, many of the poems could rightly be placed in more than one category, but they couldn't be everywhere at once.

Finally, I want this book to be an opportunity for the reader to indulge in a colourful orgy of verse that has been tucked away by academics into libraries, and by concerned parents into the backs of wardrobes, for far, far too long.

ATTRACTION

'Her amorous spicy nest'
Thomas Carew

Delight in disorder

A sweet disorder in the dress
Kindles in clothes a wantonness:
A lawn about the shoulders thrown
Into a fine distraction,
An erring lace, which here and there
Enthralls the crimson stomacher,
A cuff neglectful, and thereby
Ribbands to flow confusedly,
A winning wave (deserving note)
In the tempestuous petticoat,
A careless shoe-string, in whose tie
I see a wild civility,
Do more bewitch me, than when art
Is too precise in every part.

Robert Herrick (1591–1674)

Wasted days

(From a Picture Painted by Miss V. T.)

A fair slim boy not made for this world's pain,
With hair of gold thick clustering round his ears,
   And longing eyes half veiled by foolish tears
Like bluest water seen through mists of rain;
Pale cheeks whereon no kiss hath left its stain,
     Red under-lip drawn in for fear of Love,
     And white throat whiter than the breast of dove –
Alas! alas! if all should be in vain.
Behind, wide fields, and reapers all a-row
In heat and labour toiling wearily,
To no sweet sound of laughter or of lute.
The sun is shooting wide its crimson glow,
Still the boy dreams: nor knows that night is nigh,
And in the night-time no man gathers fruit.

Oscar Wilde (1854–1900)

The ninth secret poem

I worship your fleece which is the perfect triangle
   Of the Goddess
I am the lumberjack of the only virgin forest
   O my Eldorado
I am the only fish in your voluptuous ocean
   You my lovely Siren
I am the climber on your snowy mountains
   O my whitest Alp
I am the heavenly archer of your beautiful mouth
   O my darling quiver
I am the hauler of your midnight hair
   O lovely ship on the canal of my kisses
And the lilies of your arms are beckoning me
   O my summer garden
The fruits of your breast are ripening their honey for me
   O my sweet-smelling orchard
And I am raising you O Madeleine O my beauty above the earth
   Like the torch of all light.

Guillaume Apollinaire (1886–1918)
(Trans. Oliver Bernard)

Upon a mole in Celia's bosom

That lovely spot which thou dost see
In Celia's bosom was a bee,
Who built her amorous spicy nest
I'th'Hyblas of her either breast.
But from close ivory hives she flew
To suck the aromatic dew
Which from the neighbour vale distils,
Which parts those two twin-sister hills,
There feasting on ambrosial meat,
A rolling file of balmy sweat
(As in soft murmurs before death
Swan-like she sung) choked up her breath:
So she in water did expire,
More precious than the phoenix' fire.
    Yet still her shadow there remains
Confined to those Elysian plains,
With this strict law, that who shall lay
His bold lips on that milky way,
The sweet and smart from thence shall bring
Of the bee's honey and her sting.

Thomas Carew (1595?–1639)

The compliment

My dearest, I shall grieve thee
When I swear, yet sweet believe me,
By thine eyes – the tempting book
On which even crabbed old men look –
I swear to thee (though none abhor them)
Yet I do not love thee for them.

I do not love thee for that fair
Rich fan of thy most curious hair,
Though the wires thereof be drawn
Finer than the threads of lawn
And are softer than the leaves
On which the subtle spinner weaves.

I do not love thee for those flowers
Growing on thy cheeks (love's bowers),
Though such cunning them hath spread
None can part their white and red;
Love's golden arrows thence are shot,
Yet for them I love thee not.

I do not love thee for those soft
Red coral lips I've kissed so oft,
Nor teeth of pearl, the double guard
To speech, whence music still is heard –
Though from those lips a kiss being taken
Might tyrants melt and death awaken.

I do not love thee (O my fairest)
For that richest, for that rarest
Silver pillar which stands under
Thy round head, that globe of wonder,
Though that neck be whiter far
Than towers of polished ivory are.

I do not love thee for those mountains
Hilled with snow, whence milky fountains
(Sugared sweet, as syruped berries)
Must one day run through pipes of cherries;
O how much those breasts do move me –
Yet for them I do not love thee.

I do not love thee for that belly,
Sleek as satin, soft as jelly,
Though within that crystal round
Heaps of treasures might be found
So rich that for the least of them
A king might leave his diadem.

I do not love thee for those thighs
Whose alabaster rocks do rise
So high and even that they stand
Like sea-marks to some happy land.
Happy are those eyes have seen them;
More happy they that sail between them.

I love thee not for thy moist palm
Though the dew thereof be balm,
Nor for thy pretty leg and foot,
Although it be the precious root
On which this goodly cedar grows;
Sweet, I love thee not for those,

Nor for thy wit, though pure and quick,
Whose substance no arithmetic
Can number down; nor for those charms
Masked in thy embracing arms –
Though in them one night to lie,
Dearest, I would gladly die.

I love not for those eyes, nor hair,
Nor cheeks, nor lips, nor teeth so rare,
Nor for thy speech, thy neck, or breast,
Nor for thy belly, nor the rest,
Nor for thy hand nor foot so small –
But, wouldst thou know, dear sweet – for all.

Thomas Carew (1595?–1639)

SEDUCTION

'Raising the sweet, delicious pangs of love'
John Hopkins

The Song of Solomon

. . . Let him kiss me with the kisses of his mouth: for thy love is better than wine.

Because of the savour of thy good ointments thy name is as ointment poured forth, therefore do the virgins love thee.

Draw me, we will run after thee: the king hath brought me into his chambers: we will be glad and rejoice in thee, we will remember thy love more than wine: the upright love thee.
. . .

I have compared thee, O my love, to a company of horses in Pharaoh's chariots.

Thy cheeks are comely with rows of jewels, thy neck with chains of gold.

We will make thee borders of gold with studs of silver.

While the king sitteth at his table, my spikenard sendeth forth the smell thereof.

A bundle of myrrh is my well-beloved unto me: he shall lie all night betwixt my breasts.

My beloved is unto me as a cluster of camphire in the vineyards of Engedi.

Behold, thou art fair, my beloved, yea, pleasant: also our bed is green.

The beams of our house are cedar, and our rafters of fir.

I am the rose of Sharon, and the lily of the valleys.

As the lily among thorns, so is my love among the daughters.

As the apple tree among the trees of the wood, so is my beloved among the sons. I sat down under his shadow with great delight, and his fruit was sweet to my taste.

He brought me to the banqueting house, and his banner over me was love.

Stay me with flagons, comfort me with apples: for I am sick of love.

His left hand is under my head, and his right hand doth embrace me.

I charge you, O ye daughters of Jerusalem, by the roes, and by the hinds of the field, that ye stir not up, nor awake my love, till he please.

The voice of my beloved! behold, he cometh leaping upon the mountains, skipping upon the hills.

My beloved is like a roe or a young hart: behold, he standeth behind our wall, he looketh forth at the windows, shewing himself through the lattice.

My beloved spake, and said unto me, Rise up, my love, my fair one, and come away.

For lo, the winter is past, the rain is over and gone;

The flowers appear on the earth; the time of the singing of birds is come, and the voice of the turtle is heard in our land;

The fig tree putteth forth her green figs, and the vines with the tender grape give a good smell. Arise, my love, my fair one, and come away.

O my dove, that art in the clefts of the rock, in the secret places of the stairs, let me see thy countenance, let me hear thy voice: for sweet is the voice, and thy countenance is comely.

The Song of Solomon 182

Ballata concerning a shepherd-maid

Within a copse I met a shepherd-maid,
More fair, I said, than any star to see.

She came with waving tresses pale and bright,
    With rosy cheer, and loving eyes of flame,
Guiding the lambs beneath her wand aright.
    Her naked feet still had the dews on them,
    As, singing like a lover, so she came;
Joyful, and fashioned for all ecstasy.

I greeted her at once, and question made
    What escort had she through the woods in spring?
But with soft accents she replied and said
    That she was all alone there, wandering;
    Moreover: 'Do you know, when the birds sing,
My heart's desire is for a mate,' said she.

While she was telling me this wish of hers,
    The birds were all in song throughout the wood.
'Even now then,' said my thought, 'the time recurs,
    With mine own longing, to assuage her mood.'
    And so, in her sweet favour's name, I sued
That she would kiss there and embrace with me.

She took my hand to her with amorous will,
    And answered that she gave me all her heart,
And drew me where the leaf is fresh and still,
    Where spring the wood-flowers in the shade apart.
    And on that day, by Joy's enchanted art,
There Love in very presence seemed to be.

Guido Cavalcanti (13th c.)
(Trans. D. G. Rossetti)

To Amasia, tickling a gentleman

Methinks I see how the blessed swain was laid
While round his sides your nimble fingers played.
With pleasing softness did they swiftly rove,
Raising the sweet, delicious pangs of love,
While at each touch they made his heart-strings move.
As round his breast, his ravished breast, they crowd,
We hear their music, when he laughs aloud.
You ply him still, and as he melting lies
Act your soft triumphs while your captive dies.
Thus he perceives, thou, dearest, charming fair
Without your eyes you can o'ercome him there.
Thus too he shows what's your unbounded skill,
You please and charm us, though at once you kill.
Lodged in your arms he does in transport lie,
While through his veins the fancied lightnings fly
And, gushed with vast delights, I see him haste to die.

John Hopkins (fl. 1700)

The geranium

In the close covert of a grove
By nature formed for scenes of love,
Said Susan in a lucky hour:
'Observe yon sweet geranium flower.
How straight upon its stalk it stands,
And tempts our violating hands,
Whilst the soft bud, as yet unspread,
Hangs down its pale declining head.
Yet soon as it is ripe to blow,
The stems shall rise, the head shall glow.'
'Nature,' said I, 'my lovely Sue,
To all her followers lends a clue.
Her simple laws themselves explain
As links of one continued chain;
For her the mysteries of creation
Are but the works of generation.
Yon blushing, strong, triumphant flower
Is in the crisis of its power;
But short, alas, its vigorous reign;
He sheds his seed, and drops again.
The bud that hangs in pale decay
Feels not, as yet, the plastic ray.
Tomorrow's sun shall make him rise,
Then, too, he sheds his seed, and dies.
But words, my love, are vain and weak;
For proof, let bright example speak.'
Then straight before the wondering maid
The tree of life I gently laid.
'Observe, sweet Sue, his drooping head,
How pale, how languid, and how dead.
Yet let the sun of thy bright eyes
Shine but a moment, it shall rise.
Let but the dew of thy soft hand
Refresh the stem, it straight shall stand.
Already, see, it swells, it grows,
Its head is redder than the rose,
Its shrivelled fruit, of dusky hue,

Now glows – a present fit for Sue.
The balm of life each artery fills,
And in o'erflowing drops distils.'
'Oh me!' cried Susan, 'When is this?
What strange tumultuous throbs of bliss!
Sure, never mortal till this hour
Felt such emotion at a flower!
Oh, serpent, cunning to deceive,
Sure 'tis this tree that tempted Eve.
The crimson apples hang so fair
Alas! what woman could forbear?'
'Well hast though guessed, my love,' I cried,
'It is the tree by which she died –
The tree which could content her.
All nature, Susan, seeks the centre.
Yet let us still poor Eve forgive,
It's the tree by which we live.
For lovely women still it grows,
And in the centre only blows.
But chief for thee it spreads its charms,
For paradise is in thy arms . . .'
I ceased, for nature kindly here
Began to whisper in her ear,
And lovely Sue lay softly panting
While the geranium tree was planting,
'Till in the heat of amorous strife
She burst the mellow tree of life.
'Oh, heaven!' cried Susan with a sigh,
'The hour we taste – we surely die.
Strange raptures seize my fainting frame,
And all my body glows with flame.
Yet let me snatch one parting kiss
To tell my love I die with bliss –
That pleased thy Susan yields her breath;
Oh, who would live, if this be death?'

Richard Brinsley Sheridan (1751–1816)

Be quiet, Sir!

Be quiet, Sir! begone, I say!
Lord bless us! How you romp and tear!
  There!
  I swear!
Now you left my bosom bare!
I do not like such boisterous play,
So take that saucy hand away –
Why now, you're ruder than before!
Nay, I'll be hanged if I comply –
  Fie!
  I'll cry!
Oh – I can't bear it – I shall die!
I vow I'll never see you more!
But – are you sure you've shut the door?

Anon (18th c.)

Sylvia the fair

Sylvia the fair, in the bloom of fifteen
Felt an innocent warmth, as she lay on the green:
She had heard of a pleasure, and something she guessed
By the towzing and tumbling and touching her breast:
She saw the men eager, but was at a loss,
What they meant by their sighing and kissing so close;
　　By their praying and whining,
　　And clasping and twining,
　　And panting and wishing,
　　And sighing and kissing,
　　And sighing and kissing so close.

Ah she cried, ah for a languishing maid
In a country of Christians to die without aid!
Not a Whig, or a Tory, or trimmer at least,
Or a Protestant parson or Catholic priest,
To instruct a young virgin that is at a loss
What they meant by their sighing and kissing so close;
　　By their praying and whining,
　　And clasping and twining,
　　And panting and wishing,
　　And sighing and kissing,
　　And sighing and kissing so close.

Cupid in shape of a swain did appear,
He saw the sad wound, and in pity drew near,
Then he showed her his arrow, and bid her not fear,
For the pain was no more than a maiden may bear;
When the balm was infused, she was not at a loss
What they meant by their sighing and kissing so close;
　　By their praying and whining,
　　And clasping and twining,
　　And panting and wishing,
　　And sighing and kissing,
　　And sighing and kissing so close.

John Dryden (1631–1700)

A lover out of fashion

Faith, wench, I cannot court thy sprightly eyes
With the base viol placed between my thighs;
I cannot lisp, nor to some fiddle sing,
Nor run upon a high stretched minikin.

I cannot whine in puling elegies
Entombing Cupid with sad obsequies.
I am not fashioned for these amorous times
To court thy beauty with lascivious rhymes.

I cannot dally, caper, dance and sing,
Oiling my saint with supple sonneting.
I cannot cross my arms, or sigh 'Ah, me –
Ah, me, forlorn!' – egregious foppery.

I cannot buss thy fist, play with thy hair,
Swearing by Jove thou art most debonaire.
Not I, by cock; but shall I tell thee roundly,
Hark in thine ear: zounds, I can swive thee soundly.

Sir John Davies (1569–1626)

A young violinist from Rio

A young violinist from Rio
Was seducing a lady named Cleo.
    As she slipped off her panties
    She said, 'No andantes;
I want this *allegro con brio*!'

                                        Anon

THE DEED

'Panting, stretching, sweating, cooing
All in the ecstasy of doing!'

Sir Charles Sedley

from Don Juan, Canto II

. . . In hollow halls, with sparry roofs and cells,
They turned to rest; and, each clasped by an arm,
Yielded to the deep twilight's purple charm.

They looked up to the sky, whose floating glow
    Spread like a rosy ocean, vast and bright;
They gazed upon the glittering sea below,
    Whence the broad moon rose circling into sight;
They heard the waves splash, and the wind so low,
    And saw each other's dark eyes darting light
Into each other — and, beholding this,
Their lips drew near, and clung into a kiss;

A long, long kiss, a kiss of youth, and love,
    And beauty, all concentrating like rays
Into one focus, kindled from above;
    Such kisses as belong to early days,
Where heart, and soul, and sense, in concert move,
    And the blood's lava, and the pulse a blaze,
Each kiss a heart-quake — for a kiss's strength,
I think, it must be reckoned by its length.

By length, I mean duration; theirs endured
    Heaven knows how long — no doubt they never reckoned;
And if they had, they could not have secured
    The sum of their sensations to a second:
They had not spoken; but they felt allured,
    As if their souls and lips each other beckoned,
Which, being joined, like swarming bees they clung —
Their hearts the flowers from whence the honey sprung.

They were alone, but not alone as they
  Who shut in chambers think it loneliness;
The silent ocean, and the starlit bay,
  The twilight glow, which momently grew less,
The voiceless sands, and dropping caves, that lay
  Around them, made them to each other press,
As if there were no life beneath the sky
Save theirs, and that their life could never die.

They feared no eyes nor ears on that lone beach,
  They felt no terrors from the night; they were
All in all to each other; though their speech
  Was broken words, they *thought* a language there –
And all the burning tongues the passions teach
  Found in one sigh the best interpreter
Of nature's oracle – first love – that all
Which Eve has left her daughters since her fall.

George Gordon, Lord Byron (1788–1824)

may i feel said he

may i feel said he
(i'll squeal said she
just once said he)
it's fun said she

(may i touch said he
how much said she
a lot said he)
why not said she

(let's go said he
not too far said she
what's too far said he
where you are said she)

may I stay said he
(which way said she
like this said he
if you kiss said she

may I move said he
is it love said she)
if you're willing said he
(but you're killing said she

but it's life said he
but your wife said she
now said he)
ow said she

(tiptop said he
don't stop said she
oh no said he)
go slow said she

(cccome? said he
ummm said she)
you're divine! said he
(you are Mine said she)

e. e. cummings
(1894–1962)

Sonnet LXIV

Coming to kiss her lips such grace I found
Me seemed I smelt a garden of sweet flowers:
That dainty odours from them threw around
For damsels fit to deck their lovers' bowers.
Her lips did smell like unto gillyflowers,
Her ruddy cheeks like unto roses red,
Her snowy brows like budded bellamours,
Her lovely eyes like pinks but newly spread,
Her goodly bosom like a strawberry bed,
Her neck like to a bunch of columbines,
Her breast like lilies, ere their leaves be shed,
Her nipples like young blossomed jessemines.
Such fragrant flowers do give most odorous smell,
But her sweet odour did them all excell.

Edmund Spenser (1552?–99)

Clothes do but cheat and cozen us

Away with silks, away with lawn,
I'll have no scenes or curtains drawn;
Give me my mistress as she is,
Dressed in her naked simplicities:
For as my heart, even so my eye
Is won with flesh, not drapery.

Robert Herrick (1591—1674)

from The platonic blow

Mad to be had, to be felt and smelled. My lips
Explored the adorable masculine tits. My eyes
Assessed the chest I caressed the athletic hips
And the slim limbs. I approved the grooves of the thighs.

I hugged, I snuggled into an armpit, I sniffed
The subtle whiff of its tuft, I lapped up the taste
Of his hot hollow. My fingers began to drift
On a trek of inspection, a leisurely tour of the waist.

Downward in narrowing circles they playfully strayed,
Encroached on his privates like poachers, approached the prick.
But teasingly swerved, retreating from the meeting. It betrayed
Its pleading need by a pretty imploring kick.

'Shall I rim you' I whispered. He shifted his limbs in assent,
Turned on his side and opened his legs, let me pass
To the dark parks behind. I kissed as I went
The great thick cord that ran from his balls to his arse.

Prying the buttocks aside, I nosed my way in
Down the shaggy slopes. I came to the puckered goal.
It was quick to my licking. He pressed his crotch to my chin.
His thighs squirmed as my tongue wormed in his hole.

His sensation yearned for consummation. He untucked
His legs and lay panting, hot as a teen-age boy
Naked, enlarged, charged, aching to get sucked,
Clawing the sheet, all his pores open to joy.

I inspected his erection. I surveyed his parts with a stare
From scrotum level. Sighting alongside the underside
Of his cock I looked through the forest of pubic hair
To the range of his chest beyond, rising lofty and wide.

I admired the texture, the delicate wrinkles and the neat
Sutures of the capacious bag. I adored the grace
Of the male genitalia. I raised the delicious meat
Up to my mouth, brought the face of its hard-on to my face.

Slipping my lips round the Byzantine dome of its head
With the tip of my tongue I caressed the sensitive groove,
He thrilled to the thrill. 'That's lovely!' he hoarsely said,
'Go on! Go on!' Very slowly I started to move.

Gently, intently, I slid to the massive base
Of the tower of power, paused there a moment down
In the warm moist thicket, then began to retrace
Inch by inch the smooth way to the throbbing crown.

Indwelling excitements swelled at delights to come
As I descended and ascended those thick distended walls.
I grasped his root between left forefinger and thumb
And with my right hand tickled his heavy voluminous balls.

I plunged with a rhythmical lunge, steady and slow
And at every stroke made a corkscrew roll with my tongue.
His soul reeled in the feeling. He whimpered 'Oh!'
As I tongued and squeezed and rolled and tickled and swung.

Then I pressed on the spot where the groin is joined to the cock,
Slipped a finger into his arse and massaged him from inside.
The secret sluices of his juices began to unlock.
He melted into what he felt. 'O Jesus!' he cried.

Waves of immeasurable pleasures mounted his member in quick
Spasms. I lay still in the north of his crotch inhaling his sweat.
His ring convulsed round my finger. Into me, rich and thick,
His hot spunk spouted in gouts, spouted in jet after jet.

W. H. Auden (1907–73)

To his mistress going to bed

Come, Madam, come, all rest my powers defy,
Until I labour, I in labour lie.
The foe oft-times having the foe in sight,
Is tired with standing though he never fight.
Off with that girdle, like heaven's zone glistering,
But a far fairer world encompassing.
Unpin that 'spangled' breastplate which you wear,
That th' eyes of busy fools may be stopped there.
Unlace yourself, for that harmonious chime
Tells me from you, that now it is bed time.
Off with that happy busk, which I envy,
That still can be, and still can stand so nigh.
Your gown going off, such beauteous state reveals,
As when from flowery meads th' hill's shadow steals.
Off with that wiry coronet and show
The hairy diadem which on you doth grow:
Now off with those shoes, and then safely tread
In this love's hallowed temple, this soft bed.
In such white robes heaven's angels used to be
Received by men; thou angel bring'st with thee
A heaven like Mahomet's paradise; and though
Ill spirits walk in white, we easily know
By this these angels from an evil sprite,
Those set our hairs, but these our flesh upright.
   Licence my roving hands, and let them go
Before, behind, between, above, below.
O my America! my new found land,
My kingdom, safeliest when with one man manned,
My mine of precious stones, my empery,
How blessed am I in this discovering thee!
To enter in these bonds, is to be free;
Then where my hand is set, my seal shall be.
   Full nakedness! all joys are due to thee.
As souls unbodied, bodies unclothed must be,
To taste whole joys. Gems which you women use
Are like Atlanta's balls, cast in men's views,
That when a fool's eye lighteth on a gem,

His earthly soul may covet theirs, not them.
Like pictures, or like books' gay coverings made
For laymen, are all women thus arrayed;
Themselves are mystic books, which only we
(Whom their imputed grace will dignify)
Must see revealed. Then since I may know,
As liberally, as to a midwife, show
Thyself: cast all, yea, this white linen hence,
Here is no penance, much less innocence.

To teach thee, I am naked first; why then
What needst thou have more covering than a man.

John Donne (1573–1631)

from The delights of Venus

Naked I lay, clasped in my Callus' arms,
Dreading, yet longing for his sweetening charms;
Two burning tapers spread around their light,
And chased away the darkness of the night,
When Callus from my panting bosom flew,
And with him from the bed, the bed cloaths drew.
I to conceal my naked body tried,
And what he wished to see, I strove to hide;
But what I held, with force he pulled away,
I blushed, but yet my thoughts were pleased to find
Myself so laid, and him I loved, so kind.
Struggling I lay, exposed to his eyes;
He viewed my breast, my belly, and my thighs,
And every part that there adjacent lies.
No part, or limb, his eager eyes escaped,
Nay my plump buttocks too he saw and clasped.
He dallied thus, thus raised the lustful fire
'Till modesty was vanquished by desire.
I then looked up, which yet I had not done,
And saw his body naked as my own;
I saw his prick with active vigour strong,
Thick as my arm, and, 'faith, almost as long,
Of cruel smart I knew I should not fail,
Because his prick so large, my cunt so small.
He soon perceived my blushings and surprise,
And straight my hand unto his prick did seize;
Which bigger grew, and did more stiffly stand,
Feeling the warmth of my enlivening hand.
Thus far I've told of the pleasing sight;
You know that prick our darling favourite.
    It is defined, a hollow boneless part
Of better use, and nobler than the heart;
With mouth, but without eyes; it has a head;
Soft as the lips, and as the cherry red;
The balls hang dangling in their hairy cods
From whence proceed the spring of tickling floods,
Good pricks should be both thick as well as tall,

Your French dildoes are a size too small.
At first they're hardly in our cunts contained;
For maidenheads are by much labour gained;
But men, well furnished with stout pricks, are wont
To force their passage thro' a bleeding cunt.
Man's unesteemed, a hated monster made,
When his prick's short, and can't for favour plead.
Women do not the man, but pintle wed;
For marriage joys are centred in the bed.
Now Callus stroked and kissed my milk-white breast,
He fell, and saw the beauties of the rest;
Stroking my belly down, he did descend
To the loved place where all his joys must end.
He seized my cunt, and gently pulled the hair;
At that I trembled; there began my fear.
My soft and yielding thighs he open forced;
And quite into my cunt his finger thrust;
With which he groped, and searched my cunt all round,
And of a maid the certain tokens found.
Then wide as could be stretched, my thighs he spread,
Under my buttocks too a pillow laid,
And told me then the fairest mark was made.
Then prostrate threw himself upon my breast
That groaned with such unusual weight opprest.
My cunt's plump lips his finger drew aside,
And then to enter, but in vain, he tried:
His body nimbly up and down he moved,
Against my cunt his tarse stood.
Sharp was the pain I suffered, yet I bor't,
Resolving not to interrupt the sport;
When suddenly I felt the tickling seed
O'erflow my cunt, my belly, and the bed.
I saw his prick, when Callus from me rose.
Limber and weak hang down his snotty nose;
For when they fuck, their stiffness then they lose,
But soon my Callus fixed his launce upright,
Raised by my hand, again prepared to fight;
Tho' then within my cunt he could not spend,
Oft times he swore the error he would mend,
And the warm juice thro' every passage send.

About my cunt I felt a burning pain,
Yet longed with more success to try again.
Callus once more new mounted to begin,
Gave me his prick, and begged I'd put it in.
At first against such impudence I railed,
But he with moving arguments prevailed.
He kissed and prayed and would not be denied,
And said prick's blind, and needs must have a guide.
Where there's no path, no track, he runs astray;
But in a beaten road can find his way.
I put it in, and made the passage stretch,
Whilst he pushed on, t'enlarge the narrow breach,
His prick bore forward with such strength and power,
That 'twould have made a cunt had there been none before.
When half was in, and but one half remained,
I sighed aloud, and of the smart complained
As he pushed down, the pain I sharper found,
And drew his weapon from my bleeding wound.
Callus is vexed to lose his half-won prize,
And spews his juicy seed upon my thighs.
My hand upon my mangled cunt I laid
To feel the monstrous wound his prick had made.

Then from the window he an ointment brought,
Which his too hasty passion had forgot.
His prick smelt sweet with what he rubbed upon't,
And seemed as fitting for my mouth as cunt.
As soon as this was done, he made me rise,
And place myself upon my hands and thighs.
My head down stooping on the bed did lie,
But my round buttocks lifted were on high,
Just like a cannon placed against the sky.
My bloody smock he then turned up behind,
As if to bugger me he had designed:
Then with his sweet and slippery prick drew near,
And vig'rously he charged me in the rear.
His prick, as soon as to my cunt applied,
Up to the hilt into my cunt did slide.
He fucked, and asked me if my cunt was sore?
Or his prick hurt me as it did before:

I answered, No, my dear; no, do not cease;
But oh! do thus as long as e'er you please.
This stroke did fully answer our intent
For at one moment both together spent
Just as we fucked, I cried, I faint, I die,
And fell down in a blissful ecstasy,
Kind Callus then drew out his prick, and said,
There, pretty fool, you've lost your maidenhead.

Now Callus had his rampant Fury laid,
And limber prick hung down his dangling head.
Since made a perfect woman, prick and I
Arrived at much familiarity.
But languishing poor prick could do no more;
Tho' not for want of will, but want of power.

Meursius (17th c.)

Amyntas led me to a grove

Amyntas led me to a grove,
   Where all the trees did shade us;
The Sun itself, though it had strove,
   Yet could not have betrayed us.
The place secure from human eyes,
   No other fear allows,
But when the winds that gently rise
   Do kiss the yielding boughs.

Down there we sat upon the moss,
   And did begin to play
A thousand wanton tricks, to pass
   The heat of all the day.
A many kisses he did give,
   And I returned the same:
Which made me willing to receive
   That which I dare not name.

His charming eyes no aid required,
   To tell their amorous tale;
On her that was already fired,
   'Twas easy to prevail.
He did but kiss, and clasp me round,
   Whilst they his thoughts expressed,
And laid me gently on the ground;
Ah! who can guess the rest?

Aphra Behn (1640–89)

Doing, a filthy pleasure is, and short

Doing, a filthy pleasure is, and short;
And done, we straight repent us of the sport:
Let us not then rush blindly on unto it,
Like lustful beasts, that only know to do it:
For lust will languish, and that heat decay,
But thus, thus, keeping endless Holy-day,
Let us together closely lie, and kiss,
There is no labour, nor no shame in this;
This hath pleased, doth please, and long will please; never
Can this decay, but is beginning ever.

Petronius (1st c. AD)
(Trans. Ben Johnson)

On fruition

None but a muse in love can tell
The sweet, tumultuous joys I feel
When on Celia's breast I lie,
When I tremble, faint and die,

Mingling kisses with embraces,
Darting tongues and joining faces,
Panting, stretching, sweating, cooing
All in the ecstasy of doing.

Sir Charles Sedley (1639?–1701)

To his coy mistress

Had we but world enough, and time,
This coyness, Lady, were no crime.
We would sit down, and think which way
To walk, and pass our long love's day.
Thou by the Indian Ganges' side
Shouldst rubies find: I by the tide
Of Humber would complain. I would
Love you ten years before the flood:
And you should, if you please, refuse
Till the conversion of the Jews.
My vegetable love should grow
Vaster than empires, and more slow.
A hundred years should go to praise
Thine eyes, and on thy forehead gaze.
Two hundred to adore each breast:
But thirty thousand to the rest.
An age at least to every part,
And the last age should show your heart:
For, Lady, you desire this state;
Nor would I love at lower rate.
    But at my back I always hear
Time's wingèd chariot hurrying near:
And yonder all before us lie
Deserts of vast eternity.
Thy beauty shall no more be found;
Nor in thy marble vault, shall sound
My echoing song: then worms shall try
That long preserved virginity:
And your quaint honour turn to dust;
And into ashes all my lust.
The grave's a fine and private place,
But none, I think, do there embrace.

    Now, therefore, while the youthful hue
Sits on thy skin like morning dew,
And while thy willing soul transpires
At every pore with instant fires,

Now let us sport us while we may;
And now, like amorous birds of prey,
Rather at once our time devour,
Than languish in his slow-chapped power.
Let us roll all our strength, and all
Our sweetness, up into one ball:
And tear our pleasures with rough strife,
Thorough the iron gates of life.
Thus, though we cannot make our sun
Stand still, yet we will make him run.

Andrew Marvell (1621–78)

Dainty darling

Dainty darling, kind and free,
Fairest maid I ever see,
Dear, vouchsafe to look on me –
Listen when I sing to thee
    What I will do
    With a dildo:
    Sing, do with a dildo.*

Sweet, now go not yet, I pray;
Let no doubt thy mind dismay.
Here with me thou shalt but stay –
Only till I can display
    What I will do
    With a dildo:
    Sing, do with a dildo.

Quickly, prithee, now be still:
'Nay, you shall not have your will.
Trow, you men will maidens kill!'
Tarry but to learn the skill
    What I will do
    With a dildo:
    Sing, do with a dildo.

Pretty, witty, sit me by;
Fear no cast of any eye.
We will pray so privily
None shall see but you and I
    What I will do
    With a dildo:
    Sing, do with a dildo.

Anon (c. 1600)

* Still a penis in the 17th century.

from Metamorphoses, Book IV

The boy now fancies all the danger over,
And innocently sports about the shore,
Playful and wanton to the stream he trips,
And dips his foot, and shivers as he dips.
The coolness pleased him, and with eager haste
His airy garments on the banks he cast;
His godlike features, and his heavenly hue,
And all his beauties were exposed to view.
His naked limbs the nymph with rapture spies,
While hotter passions in her bosom rise,
Flush in her cheeks, and sparkle in her eyes.
She longs, she burns to clasp him in her arms,
And looks, and sighs, and kindles at his charms.

Now all undressed upon the banks he stood,
And clapped his sides, and leaped into the flood:
His lovely limbs the silver waves divide,
His limbs appear more lovely through the tide;
As lilies shut within a crystal case,
Receive a glossy lustre from the glass.
'He's mine, he's all my own', the Naiad cries,
And flings off all, and after him she flies.
And now she fastens on him as he swims,
And holds him close, and wraps about his limbs.
The more the boy resisted, and was coy,
The more she clutched, and kissed the struggling boy.
So when the wriggling snake is snatched on high
In eagle's claws, and hisses in the sky,
Around the foe his twirling tail he flings,
And twists her legs, and writhes about her wings.

The restless boy still obstinately strove
To free himself, and still refused her love.
Amidst his limbs she kept her limbs entwined,
'And why, coy youth', she cries, 'why thus unkind?
Oh may the Gods thus keep us ever joined!

Oh may we never, never, never part again!'
So prayed the nymph, nor did she pray in vain:
For now she finds him, as his limbs she pressed,
Grow nearer still, and nearer to her breast;
Till, piercing each other's flesh, they run
Together, and incorporate in one:
Last in one face are both their faces joined,
As when the stock and grafted twig combined
Shoot up the same, and wear a common rind:
Both bodies in a single body mix,
A single body with a double sex.

Ovid (43 BC–AD 18)
(Trans. Joseph Addison)

46

from De rerum natura, Book IV

. . . Of like importance is the posture too,
In which the genial feat of Love we do:
For as the females of the four foot kind,
Receive the leapings of their males behind;
So the good wives, with loins uplifted high,
And leaning on their hands the fruitful stroke may try:
For in that posture will they best conceive:
Not when supinely laid they frisk and heave;
For active motions only break the blow,
And more of strumpets than of wives they show;
When answering stroke with stroke, the mingled liquors flow.
Endearments eager, and too brisk a bound,
Throws off the plow-share from the furrowed ground.
But common harlots in conjunction heave,
Because 'tis less their business to conceive
Than to delight, and to provoke the deed;
A trick which honest wives but little need.
Nor is it from the gods, or Cupid's dart,
That many a homely woman takes the heart;
But wives well humoured, dutiful, and chaste,
And clean, will hold their wand'ring husbands fast,
Such are the links of love, and such a love will last.
For what remains, long habitude, and use,
Will kindness in domestic bands produce:
For custome will a strong impression leave;
Hard bodies, which the lightest stroke receive,
In length of time, will moulder and decay,
And stones with drops of rain are washed away.

Lucretius (c. 99–55 BC)
(Trans. John Dryden)

Corydon and Phyllis

Young Corydon and Phyllis
Sat in a lovely grove;
Contriving crowns of lilies,
Repeating tales of love,
And something else, but what I dare not name.

But as they were a-playing,
She ogled so the swain;
It saved her plainly saying
Let's kiss to ease our pain:
And something else, but what I dare not name.

A thousand times he kissed her,
Laying her on the green;
But as he farther pressed her,
A pretty leg was seen:
And something else, but what I dare not name.

So many beauties viewing,
His ardour still increased;
And greater joys pursuing,
He wandered over her breast:
And something else, but what I dare not name.

A last effort she trying,
His passion to withstand;
Cried (but it was faintly crying)
Pray take away your hand:
And something else, but what I dare not name.

Young Corydon grown bolder,
The minutes would improve;
This is the time, he told her,
To show you how I love;
And something else, but what I dare not name.

The nymph seemed almost dying,
Dissolved in amorous heat;
She kissed and told him sighing,
My dear your love is great:
And something else, but what I dare not name.

But Phyllis did recover
Much sooner than the swain;
She blushing asked her lover,
Shall we not kiss again:
And something else, but what I dare not name.

Thus Love his revels keeping,
'Til Nature at a stand;
From talk they fell to sleeping,
Holding each other's hand;
And something else, but what I dare not name.

Sir Charles Sedley (1639?–1701)

Blessed as the immortal gods

Blessed as the immortal Gods is he,
The youth who fondly sits by thee,
And hears and sees thee all the while
Softly speak and sweetly smile.

'Twas this deprived my soul of rest,
And raised such tumults in my breast;
For while I gazed, in transport tossed,
My breath was gone, my voice was lost.

My bosom glowed: the subtle flame
Ran quick through all my vital frame;
O'er my dim eyes a darkness hung;
My ears with hollow murmurs rung.

In dewy damps my limbs were chilled;
My blood with gentle horrors thrilled;
My feeble pulse forgot to play –
I fainted, sunk and died away.

Sappho (c. mid–7th c. BC)
(Trans. Ambrose Philips)

As I was walking

As I was walking down the town
I saw two people lying down.
Her skirt was up,
his arse was bare
I saw the flesh beneath the hair.
His balls they twangled to and fro
if that's not fucking, I don't know.

Anon

In days of old when knights were bold

In days of old when knights were bold
and condoms weren't invented
    they wrapped their socks
    around their cocks
and babies were prevented.

Anon

According to old Sigmund Freud

According to old Sigmund Freud,
Life is seldom so well enjoyed
    As in human coition
    (In any position)
With the usual organs employed.

Anon

There was a young plumber of Leigh

There was a young plumber of Leigh
Was plumbing a maid by the sea.
    Said the maid, 'Cease your plumbing,
    I think someone's coming.'
Said the plumber, still plumbing, 'It's me.'

Attributed to Arnold Bennett (1867–1931)

A BIT OF
THE OTHER

'Oh darling, what heaven, how did you think
Of doing that?'

Stevie Smith

Something of a departure

Would you be an angel
And let me rest,
This one last time,
Near that plum-coloured beauty spot
Just below your right buttock?

Elizabeth, Elizabeth,
Had words not escaped us both
I would have liked to hear you sing
Farewell to Tarwathie
Or *Ramble Away*.

Your thigh, your breast,
Your wrist, the ankle
That might yet sprout a wing –
You're altogether as slim
As the chance of our meeting again.

So put your best foot forward
And steady, steady on.
Show me the plum-coloured beauty spot
Just below your right buttock,
And take it like a man.

Paul Muldoon (1951–)

from The delights of Venus

Tullia replies, my dear Octavia, you,
That I can teach, shall every secret know.
Come this way, I've a pretty engine here,
Which used to ease the torments of the fair;
And next those joys which charming Man can give,
This best a woman's passion can relieve.
This dildo 'tis, with which I oft was wont
To assuage the raging of my lustful cunt.
For when cunts swell, and glow with strong desire,
'Tis only pricks can quench the lustful fire;
And when that's wanting, dildoes must supply
The place of pricks upon necessity.
Then on your back lie down upon the bed,
And lift your petticoats above your head;
I'll show you a new piece of lechery,
For I'll the man, you shall the woman be.
Your thin transparent smock, my dear remove
That last blessed cover to the scene of love,
What's this I see, you fill me with surprise,
Your charming beauties dazzle quite my eyes!
Gods! what a leg is here! what lovely thighs!
A belly too, as polished ivory white,
And then a cunt would charm an anchorite!
Oh! now I wish I were a man indeed,
That I might gain thy pretty maidenhead,
But since, my dear, I can't my wish obtain,
Let's now proceed to instruct you in the game;
That game that brings the most substantial bliss;
For swiving of all games the sweetest is.
Open wide your legs, and throw them round my back,
And clasp your snowy arms about my neck.
Your buttocks then move nimbly up and down,
Whilst with my hand I thrust the dildo home.
You'll feel the titulation by and by;
Have you no pleasure yet, no tickling joy?
Oh! yes, yes, now I faint, I die.

Meursius (17th c.)

To a plum-coloured bra displayed in Marks & Spencer

The last time I saw you, as like as two pins,
you were softly supporting those heavenly twins
that my hands liberated before the gas fire
in the mounting impatience of driving desire,

when the nipples appeared with their cherry-ripe tips,
so inviting to fingers and tongues and to lips
as they hardened and pardoned my roughness and haste
and both had, like her body, a feminine taste.

You're a bra made in millions, promiscuously sold –
but your sister contained something dearer than gold.
Mass-production, seduction; you've got it all there
on that counterfeit torso so cold and so bare,

but you serve to remind me, as nothing else could,
of the heartbeats and touching, what's tender and good.
I could ikon you, candle you, kneel on the floor,
my love's symbol of richness – in all else I'm poor!

Gavin Ewart (1916–)

Song

Fair Chloris in a pigsty lay;
  Her tender herd lay by her.
She slept; in murmuring gruntlings they,
Complaining of the scorching day,
  Her slumbers thus inspire.

She dreamt whilst she with careful pains
  Her snowy arms employed
In ivory pails to fill out grains,
One of her love-convicted swains
  Thus hasting to her cried:

'Fly, nymph! Oh, fly ere 'tis too late
  A dear, loved life to save;
Rescue your bosom pig from fate
Who now expires, hung in the gate
  That leads to Flora's cave.

'Myself had tried to set him free
  Rather than brought the news,
But I am so abhorred by thee
That even thy darling's life from me
  I know thou wouldst refuse.'

Struck with the news, as quick she flies
  As blushes to her face;
Not the bright lightning from the skies,
Nor love, shot from her brighter eyes,
  Move half so swift a pace.

This plot, it seems, the lustful slave
  Had laid against her honour
Which not one god took care to save,
For he pursues her to the cave
  And throws himself upon her.

Now piercèd is her virgin zone –
   She feels the foe within it.
She hears a broken amorous groan,
The panting lover's fainting moan,
   Just in the happy minute.

Frighted she wakes, and waking frigs.
   Nature thus kindly eased
In dreams raised by her murmuring pigs
And her own thumb between her legs,
   She's innocent and pleased.

John Wilmot, Earl of Rochester (1647–80)

Gellius is thin

Gellius is thin: why not? His mom
Obliges and his charming sister too;
His uncle lets his pretty cousins come
To visit him, and he knows what to do.
His naughty prick is always getting in
Where it should not. No wonder that he's thin.

Catullus (c. 84–c. 54 BC)
(Trans. R. Meyers & R. J. Ormsby)

In Francum

When Francus comes to solace with his whore
He sends for rods and strips himself stark naked:
For his lust sleeps, and will not rise before,
By whipping of the wench it be awaked.
  I envy him not, but wish I had the power,
  To make myself his wench but one half hour.

Sir John Davies (1569–1626)

Kisses loathsome

I abhor the slimy kiss,
(Which to me most loathsome is).
Those lips please me which are placed
Close, but not too strictly laced:
Yielding I would have them; yet
Not a wimbling tongue admit:
What would poking-sticks make there,
When the ruff is set elsewhere?

Robert Herrick (1591–1674)

from Christabel

Beneath the lamp the lady bowed,
And slowly rolled her eyes around;
Then drawing in her breath aloud,
Like one that shuddered, she unbound
The cincture from beneath her breast:
Her silken robe, and inner vest,
Dropt to her feet, and full in view,
Behold! her bosom and half her side –
A sight to dream of, not to tell!
O shield her! shield sweet Christabel!

Yet Geraldine nor speaks nor stirs;
Ah! what a stricken look was hers!
Deep from within she seems half-way
To lift some weight with sick assay,
And eyes the maid and seeks delay;
Then suddenly, as one defied,
Collects herself in scorn and pride,
And lay down by the Maiden's side! –
And in her arms the maid she took,
   Ah wel-a-day!
And with low voice and doleful look
These words did say:
'In the touch of this bosom there worketh a spell,
Which is lord of thy utterance, Christabel!
Thou knowest tonight, and wilt know tomorrow,
This mark of my shame, this seal of my sorrow;
   But vainly thou warrest,
     For this is alone in
   Thy power to declare,
     That in the dim forest
   Thou heard'st a low moaning,
And found'st a bright lady, surpassingly fair;
And didst bring her home with thee in love and in charity,
To shield her and shelter her from the damp air.'

Samuel Taylor Coleridge (1772–1834)

Each man his humour hath

Each man his humour hath, and, faith, 'tis mine
To love that woman which I now define.
First I would have her wainscot foot and hand
More wrinkled far than any pleated band,
That in those furrows, if I'd take the pains,
I might both sow and reap all sorts of grains:
Her nose I'd have a foot long, not above,
With pimples embroidered, for those I love;
And at the end a comely pearl of snot,
Considering whether it should fall or not:
Provided, next, that half her teeth be out,
Nor do I care much if her pretty snout
Meet with her furrowed chin, and both together
Hem in her lips, as dry as good whit-leather:
One wall-eye she shall have, for that's a sign
In other beasts the best: why not in mine?
Her neck I'll have to be pure jet at least,
With yellow spots enamelled; and her breast,
Like a grasshopper's wing, both thin and lean,
Not to be touched for dirt, unless swept clean:
As for her belly, 'tis no matter, so
There be a belly, and a cunt also.
Yet if you will, let it be something high,
And always let there by a tympany.
But soft! where am I now? here I should stride,
Lest I fall in, the place must be so wide,
And pass unto her thighs, which shall be just
Like to an ant's that's scraping in the dust.
Into her legs I'd have love's issues fall,
And all her calf into a gouty small:
Her feet both thick and eagle-like displayed,
The symptoms of a comely, handsome maid.
As for her parts behind, I ask no more:
If they but answer those that are before,
I have my utmost wish; and, having so,
Judge whether I am happy, yea or no.

Sir John Suckling (1609–1642)

63

from Goblin market

But sweet-tooth Laura spoke in haste:
'Good folk, I have no coin;
To take were to purloin:
I have no copper in my purse,
I have no silver either,
And all my gold is on the furze
That shakes in windy weather
Above the rusty heather.'
'You have much gold upon your head,'
They answered all together:
'Buy from us with a golden curl.'
She clipped a precious golden lock,
She dropped a tear more rare than pearl,
Then sucked their fruit globes fair or red:
Sweeter than honey from the rock,
Stronger than man-rejoicing wine,
Clearer than water flowed that juice;
She never tasted such before,
How should it cloy with length of use?
She sucked and sucked and sucked the more
Fruits which that unknown orchard bore;
She sucked until her lips were sore;
Then flung the emptied rinds away
But gathered up one kernel stone,
And knew not was it night or day
As she turned home alone.

Christina Rossetti (1830–94)

Gellius, why are your lips

Gellius, why are your lips white as snow,
Which should be red, when you get up at dawn,
Or when you've had your midday nap and go
Out of your house? Those stories told in scorn
Show something's wrong; is that a truthful tale
That sucking cock is what you love to do?
Poor Victor's busted balls show why you're pale,
Your lips as well, smeared with his milked-out goo.

Catullus (c. 84–c. 54 BC)
(Trans. R. Meyers & R. J. Ormsby)

An epitaph

Here lies the amorous Fanny Hicks,
The scabbard of ten thousand pricks,
And if you wish to do her honour,
Pull out your cock, and piss upon her.

Anon

Seymour and Chantelle or Un peu de vice

In memory of A. Swinburne and Mary Gordon

Pull my arm back, Seymour,
Like the boys do,
Oh, Seymour, the pain, the pain,
Still more then, do.
I am thy schoolboy friend, now I
Am not Chantelle any more but mi.
Say 'sweet mi', 'my sweet mi'. Oh, the pain, the pain,
Kiss me and I will kiss you again.

Tell me, Seymour, when they . . . when . . .
Does it hurt as much as this
And this and this? Ah what pain.
When I do so I feel
How very painful it is for you,
No I will, so, again and again,
Now stuff the dockleaves in your mouth
And bite the pain.

Seymour, when you hold me so tight it hurts
I feel my ribs break and the blood spurt,
Oh what heaven, what bliss,
Will you kiss me, if I give you this
Kiss, and this and this? Like this?

Seymour, this morning Nanny swished me so hard
(Because I told her she had the face
Of an antediluvian animal that had
Become extinct because of being so wet)
She broke her hair-brush. What bliss.
No, don't stop me crying now with a kiss, oh God it was pain-
Ful, I could not stop crying.

Oh darling, what heaven, how did you think
Of doing that? You are my sweetest angel of a
Little cousin, and your tears
Are as nice as the sea, as icy and salt as it is.

Stevie Smith (1902–71)

from Dildoides

Dildo has nose, but cannot smell,
No stink can his great courage quell;
Nor faintly ask you what you ail;
Ere pintle, damned rogue, will do his duty,
And then sometimes he will not stand too,
Whatever his gallant or mistress can do.
    But I too long have left my heroes,
Who fell into worse hands than Nero's,
Twelve of them shut up in a box,
Martyrs as true as are in Fox
Were seized upon as goods forbidden,
Deep, under unlawful traffick hidden;
When Council grave, of deepest beard,
Were called for, out of city-herd.
But see the fate of cruel treachery,
Those goats in head, but not in lechery,
Forgetting each his wife and daughter,
Condemned these dildoes to the slaughter;
Cuckolds with rage were blinded so,
They did not their preservers know.
One less fantastic than the rest,
Stood up, and thus himself addressed:
    These dildoes may do harm, I know;
But pray what is it may not so;
Plenty has often made men proud,
And above Law advanced the crowd:
Religion's self has ruined nations,
And caused vast depopulations;
Yet no wise people ever refused it,
'Cause knaves and fools sometimes abused it.
Are you afraid, less merry griggs
Will wear false pricks like periwigs;
And being but to small ones born,
Will great ones have of wax and horn;
Since even that promotes our gain,
Methinks unjustly we complain,
If ladies rather chose to handle

Our wax in dildo than in candle,
Much good may't do 'em, so they pay for it,
And that the merchants never stay for't.
For, neighbours, is't not all one, whether
In dildoes or shoes they wear our leather?
Whether of horn they make a comb,
Or instrument to chafe the womb,
Like you, I Monsieur Dildo hate;
But the invention let's translate.
You treat 'em may like Turks or Jews,
But I'll have two for my own use,
Priapus was a Roman deity,
And much has been the world's variety,
I am resolved I'll none provoke,
From the humble garlic to the oak.
He paused, another straight steps in,
With limber prick and grisly chin,
And thus did his harangue begin:
    For soldiers, maimed by chance of war,
We artificial limbs prepare;
Why then should we bear so much spite
To lechers maimed in am'rous fight?
That what the French send for relief,
We thus condemn as witch or thief?
By dildoe, Monsieur there intends
For his French pox to make amends;
Dildoe, without the least disgrace,
May well supply the lover's place,
And make our elder girls never care for't,
Though 'twere their fortune to dance bare-foot.
Lechers, whom clap or drink disable,
Might here have dildoes to the navel.
Did not a lady of great honour
Marry a footman waiting on her?
When one of these, timely apply'd,
Had eased her lust, and saved her pride,
Safely her ladyship might have spent,
While such gallants in pocket went.
Honour itself might use the trade,
While dildo goes in masquerade.

Which of us able to prevent is
His girl from lying with his 'prentice.
Unless we other means provide
For nature to be satisfied?
And what more proper than his engine,
Which would outdo 'em, should three men join.
I therefore hold it very foolish,
Things so convenient to abolish;
Which should we burn men justly may
To that one act the ruin lay,
Of all that thrown themselves away.
  At this, all parents' hearts began
To melt apace, and not a man
In all the assembly, but found
These reasons solid were and sound.
Poor widows then with voices shrill,
And shouts of joy the hall did fill;
For wicked pricks have no mind to her,
Who has no money, nor no jointure.
  Then one in haste broke thro' the throng,
And cried aloud, are we among
Heathens or devils, to let escape us
The image of the God Priapus?
Green-sickness girls will strait adore him,
And wickedly fall down before him.
From him each superstitious hussy
Will temples make of tussy mussy.
Idolatry will fill the land,
And all true pricks forget to stand.
Curst be the wretch, who found these arts
Of losing us to women's hearts;
For will they not henceforth refuse one
When they have all that they had use on?
Or how shall I make one to pity me,
Who enjoys Man in his epitome?
Besides, what greater deviation
From sacred rights of propagation,
Than turning th'action of the pool
Whence we all come to ridicule?
The man that would have thunder made,

With brazen road, for courser made,
In my mind did not half so ill do
As he that found this wicked dildo.
Then let's with common indignation,
Now cause a sudden conflagration
Of all these instruments of lewdness;
And, ladies, take it not for rudeness;
For never was so base a treachery
Contrived by mortals against lechery,
Men would kind husbands seem, and able,
With feigned lust, and borrowed bawble.
Lovers themselves would dress their passion
In this fantastic new French fashion;
And with false heart and member too,
Rich widows for convenience woo.
But the wise City will take care,
That men shall vend no such false ware.
See now th'unstable vulgar mind
Shook like a leaf with every wind;
No sooner has he spoke, but all
With a great rage for faggots call:
The reasons which before seem'd good,
Were now no longer understood.
This last speech had the fatal power
To bring the dildoes' latest hour.
   Priapus thus, in box opprest,
   Burnt like a phoenix in her nest;
   But with this fatal difference dies,
   No dildoes from the ashes rise.

           Samuel Butler (1663?–78)

from Charmides

Long time he lay and hardly dared to breathe,
  And heard the cadenced drip of spilt-out wine,
And the rose-petals falling from the wreath
  As the night breezes wandered through the shrine,
And seemed to be in some entrancèd swoon
Till through the open roof above the full and brimming moon

Flooded with sheeny waves the marble floor,
  When from his nook up leapt the venturous lad,
And flinging wide the cedar-carven door
  Beheld an awful image saffron-clad
And armed for battle! the gaunt Griffin glared
From the huge helm, and the long lance of wreck and ruin flared

Like a red rod of flame, stony and steeled,
  The Gorgon's head its leaden eyeballs rolled,
And writhed its snaky horrors through the shield,
  And gaped aghast with bloodless lips and cold
In passion impotent, while with blind gaze
The blinking owl between the feet hooted in shrill amaze.

The lonely fisher as he trimmed his lamp
  Far out at sea off Sunium, or cast
The net for tunnies, heard a brazen tramp
  Of horses smite the waves, and a wild blast
Divide the folded curtains of the night,
And knelt upon the little poop, and prayed in holy fright.

And guilty lovers in their venery
  Forgat a little while their stolen sweets,
Deeming they heard dread Dian's bitter cry;
  And the grim watchmen on their lofty seats
Ran to their shields in haste precipitate,
Or strained black-bearded throats across the dusky parapet.

For round the temple rolled the clang of arms,
    And the twelve Gods leapt up in marble fear,
And the air quaked with dissonant alarums
    Till huge Poseidon shook his mighty spear,
And on the frieze the prancing horses neighed,
And the low tread of hurrying feet rang from the cavalcade.

Ready for death with parted lips he stood,
    And well content at such a price to see
That calm wide brow, that terrible maidenhood,
    The marvel of that pitiless chastity,
Ah! well content indeed, for never wight
Since Troy's young shepherd prince had seen so wonderful a sight.

Ready for death he stood, but lo! the air
    Grew silent, and the horses ceased to neigh,
And off his brow he tossed the clustering hair,
    And from his limbs he threw the cloak away,
For whom would not such love make desperate,
And nigher came, and touched his throat, and with hands violate

Undid the cuirass, and the crocus gown,
    And bared the breasts of polished ivory,
Till from the waist the peplos falling down
    Left visible the secret mystery
Which to no lover will Athena show,
The grand cool flanks, the crescent thighs, the bossy hills of snow.

Those who have never known a lover's sin
    Let them not read my ditty, it will be
To their dull ears so musicless and thin
    That they will have no joy of it, but ye
To whose wan cheeks now creeps the lingering smile,
Ye who have learned who Eros is, – O listen yet awhile.

A little space he let his greedy eyes
    Rest on the burnished image, till mere sight
Half swooned for surfeit of such luxuries,
    And then his lips in hungering delight
Fed on her lips, and round the towered neck
He flung his arms, nor cared at all his passion's will to check.

Never I ween did lover hold such tryst,
    For all night long he murmured honeyed word,
And saw her sweet unravished limbs, and kissed
    Her pale and argent body undisturbed,
And paddled with the polished throat, and pressed
His hot and beating heart upon her chill and icy breast.

It was as if Numidian javelins
    Pierced through and through his wild and whirling brain,
And his nerves thrilled like throbbing violins
    In exquisite pulsation, and the pain
Was such sweet anguish that he never drew
His lips from hers till overhead the lark of warning flew.

They who have never seen the daylight peer
    Into a darkened room, and drawn the curtain,
And with dull eyes and wearied from some dear
    And worshipped body risen, they for certain
Will never know of what I try to sing,
How long the last kiss was, how fond and late his lingering. . . .

Oscar Wilde (1854–1900)

74

from Don Leon

Byron's married life

That time it was, as we in parlance wiled
Away the hours, my wife was big with child.
Her waist, which looked so taper when a maid
Like some swol'n butt its bellying orb displayed,
And Love, chagrined, beheld his favourite cell
From mounds opposing scarce accessible.
'Look, Bell,' I cried; 'yon moon, which just now rose
Will be the ninth; and your parturient throes
May soon Lucina's dainty hand require
To make a nurse of thee, of me a sire.
I burn to press thee, but I fear to try,
Lest like an incubus my weight should lie;
Lest, from the close encounter we should doom
Thy quickening fœtus to an early tomb.
Thy size repels me, whilst thy charms invite;
Then, say, how celebrate the marriage rite?
Learn'd Galen, Celsus, and Hippocrates,
Have held it good, in knotty points like these,
Lest mischief from too rude assaults should come,
To copulate ex more pecudum.
What sayst thou, dearest? Do not cry me nay;
We cannot err where science shows the way.'
She answered not; but silence gave consent,
And by that threshold boldly in I went.
So clever statesmen, who concoct by stealth
Some weighty measures for the commonwealth,
All comers by the usual door refuse,
And let the favoured few the back stairs use.

Anon (early 19th c.)

75

There was a young student of Johns

There was a young student of John's
Who wanted to bugger the swans.
  But the loyal hall porter
  Said, 'Sir, take my daughter.
Them birds are reserved for the dons.'

Anon

There was a young fellow of Lyme

There was a young fellow of Lyme,
Who lived with three wives at one time.
  When asked: 'Why the third?'
  He replied: 'One's absurd,
And bigamy, sir, is a crime.'

Anon

The new cinematic emporium

The new cinematic emporium
Is not just a super-sensorium,
    But a highly effectual
    Heterosexual
Mutual masturbatorium.

Anon

A weakling who lacked protoplasm

A weakling who lacked protoplasm
Sought to give his young wife an orgasm,
    But his tongue jumped the gap
    'Twixt the front and the back,
And got pinched in a bad anal spasm.

Anon

A fellow with passions quite gingery

A fellow with passions quite gingery
Was exploring his young sister's lingerie;
    Then with giggles of pleasure
    He plundered her treasure –
Adding incest to insult and injury.

Anon

A short-sighted sailor from Brighton

A short-sighted sailor from Brighton
Remarked to his girl, 'You've a tight one.'
    She replied, ''Pon my soul,
    You're in the wrong hole –
There's plenty of room in the right one.'

Anon

A gay boy who lived in Khartoum

A gay boy who lived in Khartoum
Took a lesbian up to his room,
   And they argued all night
   Over who had the right
To do what, and with what, and to whom.

Anon

There was a young couple called Kelly

There was a young couple called Kelly
Who had to live belly to belly,
   For once, in their haste,
   They used library paste
Instead of petroleum jelly.

Anon

LOVE AND LUST

'I know sex isn't love,
But it's such an attractive facsimile'
Anon

Cleft for me

Ah! Cleft for me! the lover cries,
that simple girlish part
as powerful as expressive eyes
though further from the heart!
From birth ordained, o She divine,
existing only to be mine!

Existing in that little girl
beneath the tiny skirt,
as winsome as a walnut whirl,
a tireless, heartless flirt,
fashioned by Venus, made to be
open and friendly just to me!

Oh, lover, your romantic pen
has carried you away;
it has been loved by other men,
and that auspicious day
when that wet sponge assuaged your thirst
won't be the last, was not the first

Gavin Ewart (1916–)

In summer's heat

In summer's heat and mid-time of the day,
To rest my limbs upon a bed I lay,
One window shut, the other open stood,
Which gave such light as twinkles in a wood
Like twilight glimpse at setting of the sun,
Or night being past and yet not day begun.
Such light to shamefaced maidens must be shown,
Where they may sport, and seem to be unknown.
Then came Corinna in a long, loose gown,
Her white neck hid with tresses hanging down,
Resembling fair Semiramis going to bed,
Or Lais of a thousand wooers sped.
I snatched her gown, being thin the harm was small,
Yet strived she to be covered therewithal,
And, striving thus as one that would be chaste,
Betrayed herself, and yielded at the last.
Stark naked as she stood before mine eye,
Not one wen in her body could I spy.
What arms and shoulders did I touch and see?
How apt her breasts were to be pressed by me?
How smooth a belly under her waist saw I?
How large a leg, and what a lusty thigh?
To leave the rest, all liked me passing well;
I clinged her naked body, down she fell.
Judge you the rest. Being tired, she bade me kiss.
Jove send me more such afternoons as this.

Ovid (43 BC–AD 18)
(Trans. Christopher Marlowe)

An ever-fixed mark

Years ago, at a private school
Run on traditional lines,
One fellow used to perform
Prodigious feats in the dorm;
His quite undevious designs
Found many a willing tool.

On the rugger field, in the gym,
Buck marked down at his leisure
The likeliest bits of stuff;
The notion, familiar enough,
Of 'using somebody for pleasure'
Seemed handy and harmless to him.

But another chap was above
The diversions of such a lout;
Seven years in the place
And he never got to first base
With the kid he followed about:
What interested Ralph was love.

He did the whole thing in style –
Letters three times a week,
Sonnet-sequences, Sunday walks;
Then, during one of their talks,
The youngster caressed his cheek,
And that made it all worth while.

These days, for a quid pro quo,
Ralph's chum does what, and with which;
Buck's playmates, family men,
Eye a Boy Scout now and then.
Sex is a momentary itch,
Love never lets you go.

Kingsley Amis (1922–)

from De rerum natura, Book IV

When Love its utmost vigour does employ,
Even then, 'tis but a restless wandering joy:
Nor knows the lover, in that wild excess,
With hands or eyes, what first he would possess:
But strains at all; and fastening where he strains,
Too closely presses with his frantic pains:
With biting kisses hurts the twining fair,
Which shows his joys imperfect, insincere:
For stung with inward rage, he flings around,
And strives to avenge the smart on that which gave the wound.
But love those eager bitings does restrain,
And mingling pleasure, mollifies the pain.
For ardent hope still flatters anxious grief,
And sends him to his foe to seek relief:
Which yet the nature of the thing denies;
For Love, and Love alone of all our joys
By full possession does but fan the fire,
The more we still enjoy, the more we still desire.

So Love with phantoms cheats our longing eyes,
Which hourly seeing, never satisfies;
Our hands pull nothing from the parts they strain,
But wander over the lovely limbs in vain:
Nor when the youthful pair more closely join,
When hands in hands they lock, and thighs in thighs they twine;
Just in the raging foam of full desire,
When both press on, both murmur, both expire,
They grip, they squeeze, their humid tongues they dart,
As each would force their way to the other's heart:
In vain; they only cruise about the coast,
For bodies cannot pierce, nor be in bodies lost:
As sure they strive to be, when both engage,
In that tumultuous momentary rage,
So tangled in the nets of Love they lie,
Till man dissolves in that excess of joy.

Then, when the gathered bag has burst its way,
And ebbing tides the slackened nerves betray,
A pause ensues; and Nature nods a while,
Till with recruited rage new spirits boil;
And then the same vain violence returns,
With flames renewed the erected furnace burns.
Again they in each other would be lost,
But still by adamantine bars are crossed;
All ways they try, successless all they prove,
To cure the secret sore of lingering love.

Lucretius (c. 99–55 BC)
(Trans. John Dryden)

i like my body when it is with your

i like my body when it is with your
body. It is so quite new a thing.
Muscles better and nerves more.
i like your body. i like what it does,
i like its hows. i like to feel the spine
of your body and its bones, and the trembling
-firm-smooth ness and which i will
again and again and again
kiss, i like kissing this and that of you,
i like, slowly stroking the, shocking fuzz
of your electric fur, and what-is-it comes
over parting flesh. . . . And eyes big love-crumbs,

and possibly i like the thrill

of under me you so quite new

e. e. cummings (1894–1962)

A woman waits for me

A woman waits for me, she contains all, nothing is lacking,
Yet all were lacking if sex were lacking, or if the moisture of the
right man were lacking.

Sex contains all, bodies, souls,
Meanings, proofs, purities, delicacies, results, promulgations,
Songs, commands, health, pride, the maternal mystery, the
seminal milk,
All hopes, benefactions, bestowals, all the passions, loves, beauties,
delights of the earth,
All the governments, judges, gods, follow'd persons of the earth,
These are contained in sex as parts of itself and justifications of
itself.

Without shame the man I like knows and avows the deliciousness
of his sex,
Without shame the woman I like knows and avows hers.

Now I will dismiss myself from impassive women,
I will go stay with her who waits for me, and with those women
that are warm-blooded and sufficient for me,
I see that they understand me and do not deny me,
I see that they are worthy of me, I will be the robust husband of
those women.

They are not one jot less than I am,
They are tann'd in the face by shining suns and blowing winds,
Their flesh has the old divine suppleness and strength,
They know how to swim, row, ride, wrestle, shoot, run, strike,
retreat, advance, resist, defend themselves,
They are ultimate in their own right – they are calm, clear, well-
possessed of themselves.

I draw you close to me, you women,
I cannot let you go, I would do you good,
I am for you, and you are for me, not only for our own sake, but
for others' sakes,
Enveloped in you sleep greater heroes and bards,
They refuse to awake at the touch of any man but me.

It is I, you women, I make my way,
I am stern, acrid, large, undissuadable, but I love you,
I do not hurt you any more than is necessary for you,
I pour the stuff to start sons and daughters fit for these States, I
press with slow rude muscle,
I brace myself effectually, I listen to no entreaties,
I dare not withdraw till I deposit what has so long accumulated
within me.

Through you I drain the pent-up rivers of myself,
In you I wrap a thousand onward years,
On you I graft the grafts of the best-beloved of me and America,
The drops I distil upon you shall grow fierce and athletic girls,
new artists, musicians, and singers,
The babes I beget upon you are to beget babes in their turn,
I shall demand perfect men and women out of my love-
spendings,
I shall expect them to interpenetrate with others, as I and you
interpenetrate now,
I shall count on the fruits of the gushing showers of them, as I
count on the fruits of the gushing showers I give now,
I shall look for loving crops from the birth, life, death,
immortality, I plant so lovingly now.

Walt Whitman (1819–92)

Love and sleep

Lying asleep between the strokes of night
   I saw my love lean over my sad bed,
   Pale as the duskiest lily's leaf or head,
Smooth-skinned and dark, with bare throat made to bite,
Too wan for blushing and too warm for white,
   But perfect-coloured without white or red.
   And her lips opened amorously, and said –
I wist not what, saving one word – Delight.
And all her face was honey to my mouth,
   And all her body pasture to mine eyes;
     The long lithe arms and hotter hand than fire,
The quivering flanks, hair smelling of the south,
   The bright light feet, the splendid supple thighs
     And glittering eyelids of my soul's desire.

Algernon Charles Swinburne (1837–1909)

Ipsithilla, baby girl

Ipsithilla, baby girl,
Sugar, honey, let me curl
Up with you this afternoon,
Tell me that I can come soon,
Tell me none will bar your door,
That you're not busy, and what's more
That you will wait for me and choose
To give me nine successive screws.
Oh, don't delay, don't make me wait,
I'm resting, stuffed with all I ate,
Feeling my pecker stand up straight.

Catullus (c. 84–c. 54 BC)
(Trans. R. Meyers & R. J. Ormsby)

from Satires, VI

Who knows not now, my friend, the secret rites
Of the Good Goddess; when the dance excites
The boiling blood; when, to distraction wound,
By wine, and music's stimulating sound,
The maenads of Priapus, with wild air,
Howl horrible, and toss their flowing hair!
Then, how the wine at every pore o'erflows!
How the eye sparkles! how the bosom glows!
How the cheek burns! and, as the passions rise,
How the strong feeling bursts in eager cries! –
Saufeia now springs forth, and tries a fall
With the town prostitutes, and throws them all;
But yields, herself, to Medullina, known
For parts, and powers, superior to her own.
Maids, mistresses, alike the contest share,
And 'tis not always birth that triumphs there.
   Nothing is feigned in this accursed game:
'Tis genuine all; and such as would inflame
The frozen age of Priam, and inspire
The ruptured, bedrid Nestor with desire.
Stung with their mimic feats, a hollow groan
Of lust breaks forth; the sex, the sex is shown!
And one loud yell re-echoes through the den,
'Now, now, 'tis lawful! now admit the men!'
There's none arrived. 'Not yet! then scour the street,
And bring us quickly, here, the first you meet.'
There's none abroad. 'Then fetch our slaves.' They're gone.
'Then hire a waterman.' There's none. 'Not one!' –
Nature's strong barrier scarcely now restrains
The baffled fury in their boiling veins!

Juvenal (c. AD 60–136)
(Trans. William Gifford)

93

Circe

It certainly is the smell of her cunt
makes you fall on your knees and grunt.

It certainly is the slope of her tits
makes your morality fall to bits.

It certainly is her incurved waist
makes you long for that truffle taste.

It certainly is her pubic thighs
makes your piglike prick uprise.

It certainly is her heavenly hair
makes you wallow and keeps you bare.

It certainly is her beautiful bum
makes you rootle and holds you dumb.

It certainly is her feminine hands
makes you the slave of glorious glands.

It certainly is the commanding eye
makes you happy to live in a sty.

Gavin Ewart (1916–)

From I sing the body electric

This is the female form,
A divine nimbus exhales from it from head to foot,
It attracts with fierce undeniable attraction.
I am drawn by its breath as if I were no more than a helpless
vapor, all falls aside but myself and it,
Books, art, religion, time, the visible and solid earth, and what
was expected of heaven or feared of hell, are now consumed,
Mad filaments, ungovernable shoots play out of it, the response
likewise ungovernable,
Hair, bosom, hips, bend of legs, negligent falling hands all
diffused, mine too diffused,
Ebb stung by the flow and flow stung by the ebb, love-flesh
swelling and deliciously aching,
Limitless limpid jets of love hot and enormous, quivering jelly of
love, white-blow and delirious juice,
Bridegroom night of love working surely and softly into the
prostrate dawn,
Undulating into the willing and yielding day,
Lost in the cleave of the clasping and sweet-fleshed day.

Walt Whitman (1819–92)

Between your sheets

Between your sheets you soundly sleep
Nor dream of vigils that we lovers keep
While all the night, I waking sign your name,
The tender sound does every nerve inflame,
Imagination shows me all your charms,
The plenteous silken hair, and waxen arms,
The well turned neck, and snowy rising breast
And all the beauties that supinely rest
   between your sheets.

Ah Lindamira, could you see my heart,
How fond, how true, how free from fraudful art,
The warmest glances poorly do explain
The eager wish, the melting throbbing pain
Which through my very blood and soul I feel,
Which you cannot believe nor I reveal,
Which every metaphor must render less
And yet (methinks) which I could well express
   between your sheets.

Lady Mary Wortley Montagu (1689–1762)

The feel of hands

The hands explore tentatively,
two small live entities whose shapes
I have to guess at. They touch me
all, with the light of fingertips

testing each surface of each thing
found, timid as kittens with it.
I connect them with amusing
hands I have shaken by daylight.

There is a sudden transition:
they plunge together in a full
formed single fury; they are grown
to cats, hunting without scruple;

they are expert but desperate.
I am in the dark. I wonder
when they grew up. It strikes me that
I do not know whose hands they are.

Thom Gunn (1929–)

from Venus and Adonis

'Now let me say good night; and so say you;
If you will say so, you shall have a kiss.'
'Good night,' quoth she; and, ere he says adieu,
The honey fee of parting tendered is:
    Her arms do lend his neck a sweet embrace;
    Incorporate then they seem; face grows to face.

Till, breathless, he disjoined, and backward drew
The heavenly moisture, that sweet coral mouth,
Whose precious taste her thirsty lips well knew,
Whereon they surfeit, yet complain on drouth:
    He with her plenty pressed, she faint with dearth,
    Their lips together glued, fall to the earth.

Now quick desire hath caught the yielding prey,
And glutton-like she feeds, yet never filleth;
Her lips are conquerors, his lips obey,
Paying what ransom the insulter willeth;
    Whose vulture thought doth pitch the price so high,
    That she will draw his lips' rich treasure dry.

And having felt the sweetness of the spoil,
With blindfold fury she begins to forage;
Her face doth reek and smoke, her blood doth boil,
And careless lust stirs up a desperate courage;
    Planting oblivion, beating reason back,
    Forgetting shame's pure blush, and honour's wrack.

Hot, faint, and weary, with her hard embacing,
Like a wild bird being tamed with too much handling,
Or as the fleet-foot roe that's tired with chasing,
Or like the froward infant stilled with dandling,
    He now obeys, and now no more resisteth,
    While she takes all she can, not all she listeth.

What wax so frozen but dissolves with tempering,
And yields at last to every light impression?
Things out of hope are compassed oft with venturing,
Chiefly in love, whose leave exceeds commission.
    Affection faints not like a pale-faced coward,
    But then woos best, when most his choice is froward.

When he did frown, O! had she then gave over,
Such nectar from his lips she had not sucked.
Foul words and frowns must not repel a lover;
What though the rose have prickles, yet 'tis plucked.
    Were beauty under twenty locks kept fast,
    Yet love breaks, through, and picks them all at last.

For pity now she can no more detain him;
The poor fool prays her that he may depart:
She is resolved no longer to restrain him,
Bids him farewell, and look well to her heart,
    The which, by Cupid's bow she doth protest.
    He carries thence incaged in his breast.

'Sweet boy,' she says, 'this night I'll waste in sorrow,
For my sick heart commands mine eyes to watch.
Tell me, Love's master, shall we meet to-morrow?
Say, shall we? shall we? wilt thou make the match?'
    He tells her, no; to-morrow he intends
    To hunt the boar with certain of his friends.

'The boar!' quoth she, whereat a sudden pale,
Like lawn being spread upon the blushing rose,
Usurps her cheek: she trembles at his tale,
And on his neck her yoking arms she throws;
    She sinketh down, still hanging by his neck,
    He on her belly falls, she on her back.

Now is she in the very lists of love,
Her champion mounted for the hot encounter:
All is imaginary she doth prove,
He will not manage her, although he mount her;
  That worse than Tantalus' is her annoy,
  To clip Elysium, and to lack her joy.

Even as poor birds, deceived with painted grapes,
Do surfeit by the eye, and pine the maw,
Even so she languisheth in her mishaps,
As those poor birds that helpless berries saw.
  The warm effects which she in him finds missing,
  She seeks to kindle with continual kissing.

But all in vain; good queen, it will not be:
She hath assayed as much as may be proved;
Her pleading hath deserved a greater fee;
She's Love, she loves, and yet she is not loved.
  'Fie, fie!' he says, 'you crush me; let me go:
  You have no reason to withhold me so.' . . .

With this, he breaketh from the sweet embrace
Of those fair arms which bound him to her breast,
And homeward through the dark land runs apace;
Leaves Love upon her back deeply distressed.
  Look, how a bright star shooteth from the sky,
  So glides he in the night from Venus' eye. . . .

William Shakespeare (1564–1616)

From A letter from the Lord Buckhurst
to Mr George Etherege

Dreaming last night on Mrs Farley,
My prick was up this morning early;
And I was fain without my gown
To rise in the cold to get him down.
Hard shift, alas, but yet a sure,
Although it be no pleasing cure.
Of old the fair Egyptian slattern,
For luxury that had no pattern,
To fortify her Roman swinger,
Instead of nutmeg, mace and ginger,
Did spice his bowels (as story tells)
With warts of rocks and spawn of shells.
It had been happy for her Grace,
Had I been in the rascal's place;
I, who do scorn that any stone
Should raise my printle but my own,
Had laid her down on every couch
And saved her pearl and diamond brooch
Until her hot-tailed Majesty,
Being happily reclaimed by me
From all her wild expensive ways,
Had worn her gems on holidays.
But since her cunt has long done itching,
Let us discourse of modern bitching.

I must entreat you by this letter,
To inquire for whores, the more the better.
Hunger makes any man a glutton;
If Roberts, Thomas, Mrs Dutton,
Or any other bawds of note,
Inform of a fresh petticoat,
Inquire, I pray, with friendly care,
Where their respective lodgings are.
Some do compare a man to a bark –
A pretty metaphor, pray mark –

And with a long and tedious story,
Will all the tackling lay before ye:
The sails are hope, the masts desire,
Till they the gentlest reader tire.
But howsoever they keep a pudder,
I'm sure the pintle is the rudder:
powerful rudder, which of force
To town will shortly steer my course.
And if you do not there provide
A port where I may safely ride,
Landing in haste, in some foul creek,
'Tis ten to one I spring a leak.

Charles Sackville,
Lord Buckhurst (1638–1706)

from Don Leon

All ye who know what pleasure 'tis to heave
A lover's sigh, the warm caress receive
Of some fond mistress, and with anxious care
Watch every caprice, and every ailment share,
Ye only know how hard it is to cure
The burning fever of love's calenture.
Come, crabbed philosophers, and tell us why
Should men to harsh ungrateful studies fly
In search of bliss, when even a single day
Of dalliance can an age of love outweigh!
How many hours I've spent in pensive guise
To watch the mild expression of his eyes!
Or when asleep at noon, and from his mouth
His breath came sweet like odours from the south,
How long I've hung in raptures as he lay,
And silent chased the insect tribe away.
How oft at morn, when troubled by the heat,
The covering fell disordered at his feet,
I've gazed unsated at his naked charms,
And clasped him waking in my longing arms.
How oft in winter, when the sky overcast
Capped the bleak mountains, and the ruthless blast
Moaned through the trees, or lashed the surfy strand,
I've drawn myself the glove upon his hand,
Thrown over his tender limbs the rough capote,
Or tied the kerchief round his snowy throat.
How oft, when summer saw me fearless brave
With manly breast the blue transparent wave,
Another Daedalus I taught him how
With spreading arms the liquid waste to plough.
Then brought him gently to the sunny beach,
And wiped the briny moisture from his breach.

Anon (early 19th c.)

'Given faith,' sighed the vicar of Deneham

'Given faith,' sighed the vicar of Deneham,
'From the lusts of the flesh we might wean 'em;
    But the human soul sighs
    For a nice pair of thighs,
And a little of what lies between 'em.'

Anon

There was a young lady of Dover

There was a young lady of Dover
Whose passion was such that it drove her
    To cry when she came,
    'Oh dear, what a shame!
Well now we just have to start over.'

Anon

There was a young fellow of King's

There was a young fellow of King's
Who cared not for whores and such things;
   But his secret desire
   Was a boy in the choir,
With a bum like two jellies on springs.

Anon

A wanton young lady of Wimley

A wanton young lady of Wimley
Reproached for not acting primly,
   Answered: 'Heavens above!
   I know sex isn't love,
But it's such an attractive facsimile.'

Anon

Amen

Oh! cunt is a kingdom, and prick is its lord;
A whore is a slave, and her mistress a bawd;
Her quim is her freehold, which brings in her rent
Where you pay when you enter, and leave when you've spent.

Anon

FAST AND LOOSE

'I rise at eleven, I dine about two,
I get drunk before seven; and the next thing I do . . .'
John Wilmot, Earl of Rochester

Sodom, a satyr on Charles II

I' th' isle of Britain, long since famous grown
For breeding the best cunts in Christendom,
There reigns, and oh! long may he reign and thrive,
The easiest King and best-bred man alive.
Him no ambition moves to get renown
Like the French fool, that wanders up and down
Starving his people, hazarding his crown.
Peace is his aim, his gentleness is such,
And love he loves, for he loves fucking much.
   Nor are his high desires above his strength:
His sceptre and his prick are of a length;
And she may sway the one who plays with the other,
And make him little wiser than his brother.
Poor prince! thy prick, like thy buffoons at Court,
Will govern thee because it makes thee sport.
'Tis sure the sauciest prick that ever did swive,
The proudest, peremptoriest prick alive.
Though safety, law, religion, life lay on 't,
'Twould break through all to make its way to cunt.
Restless he rolls about from whore to whore,
A merry monarch, scandalous and poor.

John Wilmot, Earl of Rochester (1647–80)

Low scene

The apprentice – fifteen, ugly, not too thin,
Nice in a softish uncouth way, dull skin,
Bright deep-set eyes – blue overalls – pulls out
His springy, stiff, well-tuned, quite man-sized spout
And rams the boss's wife – big but still good,
Flopped on the bed's edge – what an attitude! –
Legs up, breasts out, one hand parting her placket.
To see him crush her arse under his jacket
And quickstep forward more than back, it's clear
He's not afraid how deep he plants his gear
Or if the lady fruits – she doesn't care –
Isn't her trusty cuckold always there? –
So when she reaches, as he shoots his goal,
That rapture of the body as a whole,
She cries, 'You've made a child, I feel it, love,
And love you more,' and after his last shove
Adds, 'Look, the christening sweets,' and squats and tries
To heft and kiss his bollocks through his flies.

Paul Verlaine (1844–96)
(Trans. Alistair Elliot)

from The priapean corpus, XXVI

Romans, I appeal to you,
for there's no end in sight
of wanton molestation
of Priapus every night
by a pack of sex-starved females,
so I beg you, operate,
and amputate my penis
or it soon may be too late.
More randy than spring sparrows,
the neighbours' girls and wives
will cause my cock to rupture –
so get ready with the knives!
I'm nearly dead already,
exhausted, sick and pale,
who once could bugger brawny thieves,
was ruddy, fit and hale.
I'm sure I've got consumption –
my prognosis isn't good:
I fall to fits of coughing
till my spittle's bright with blood.

Anon
(Trans. Eugene O'Connor)

Against an old lecher

Since thy third curing of the French infection,
Priapus hath in thee found no erection,
Yet eatest thou ringoes, and potato roots,
And caviar, but it little boots.
Besides the bed's head a bottle's lately found
Of liquor that a quart cost twenty pound:
For shame, if not more grace, yet shew more wit,
Surcease, now sin leaves thee, to follow it.
Some smile, I sigh, to see thy madness such
That that which stands not, stands thee in so much.

Sir John Harington (1561–1612)

Elegies, Book I

Your husband will be with us at the treat;
May that be the last supper he shall eat.
And am poor I, a guest invited there,
Only to see, while he may touch the fair?
To see you kiss and hug your nauseous lord,
While his lewd hand descends below the board?
Now wonder not that Hippodamia's charms,
At such a sight, the centaurs urged to arms:
That in a rage, they threw their cups aside,
Assailed the bridegroom, and would force the bride.
I am not half a horse, (I wish I were:)
Yet hardly can from you my hands forbear.
Take, then, my counsel; which, observed, may be
Of some importance both to you and me.
Be sure to come before your man be there,
There's nothing can be done, but come howe'er.
Sit next to him, (that belongs to decency;)
But tread upon my foot in passing by.
Read in my looks what silently they speak,
And slyly, with your eyes, your answer make.
My lifted eye-brow shall declare my pain,
My right-hand to his fellow shall complain.
And on the back a letter shall design;
Besides a note that shall be writ in wine.
When ever you think upon our last embrace,
With your fore-finger gently touch your face.
If any word of mine offend my dear,
Pull, with your hand, the velvet of your ear.
If you are pleased with what I do or say,
Handle your rings, or with your fingers play.
As suppliants use at altars, hold the boord
When ever you wish the Devil may take your lord.
When he fills for you, never touch the cup;
But bid the officious cuckold drink it up.
The waiter on those services employ;
Drink you, and I will snatch it from the boy:
Watching the part where your sweet mouth has been,

And thence, with eager lips, will suck it in.
If he, with clownish manners thinks it fit
To taste, and offers you the nasty bit,
Reject his greasy kindness, and restore
The unsavoury morsel he had chewed before.
Nor let his arms embrace your neck, nor rest
Your tender cheek upon his hairy brest.
Let not his hand within your bosom stray,
And rudely with your pretty bubbies play.
But, above all, let him no kiss receive;
That's an offence I never can forgive.
Do not, O do not that sweet mouth resign,
Lest I rise up in arms; and cry 'Tis mine.
I shall thrust in betwixt, and void of fear
The manifest adulterer will appear.
These things are plain to sight, but more I doubt
What you conceal beneath your petticoat.
Take not his leg between your tender thighs,
Nor with your hand, provoke my foe to rise.
How many love-inventions I deplore,
Which I, my self, have practised all before?
How oft have I been forced the robe to lift
In company; to make a homely shift
For a bare bout, ill huddled over in haste
While over my side the fair her mantle cast.
You to your husband shall not be so kind;
But, lest you should, your mantle leave behind.
Encourage him to tope, but kiss him not,
Nor mix one drop of water in his pot.
If he be fuddled well, and snores apace,
Then we may take advice from time and place.
When all depart, while complements are loud,
Be sure to mix among the thickest crowd:
There I will be, and there we cannot miss,
Perhaps to grubble, or at least to kiss.
Alas, what length of labour I employ,
Just to secure a short and transient joy!

Ovid (43 BC–AD 18)
(Trans. John Dryden)

Hye nonny nonny noe

Down lay the shepherd swain
  so sober and demure,
Wishing for his wench again
  so bonny and so pure,
With his head on hillock low
  and his arms akimbo,
And all was for the loss of his
  Hye nonny nonny noe.

His tears fell as thin
  as water from the still,
His hair upon his chin
  grew like thyme upon a hill,
His cheery cheeks pale as snow
  did testify his mickle woe,
And all was for the loss of his
  hye nonny nonny noe.

Sweet she was, as kind a love
  as ever fettered swain;
Never such a dainty one
  shall man enjoy again.
Set a thousand on a row,
  I forbid that any show
Ever the like of her
  hye nonny nonny noe.

Face she had of filbert hue
  and bosomed like a swan,
Back she had of bended ewe,
  and waisted by a span.
Hair she had as black as crow,
  from the head unto the toe,
Down down all over her
  hye nonny nonny noe.

With her mantle tucked up high
    she foddered her flock,
So buxom and alluringly
    her knee upheld her smock,
So nimbly did she use to go
    so smooth she danced on tip-toe,
That all the men were fond of her
    hye nonny nonny noe.

She smiled like a holy-day,
    she simpered like the spring,
She pranked it like a popinjay,
    and like a swallow sing:
She tripped it like a barren doe,
    She strutted like a gorcrow,
Which made the men so fond of her
    hye nonny nonny noe.

To sport it on the merry down
    to dance the lively hay;
To wrestle for a green gown
    in heat of all the day,
Never would she say me no,
    yet me thought I had though
Never enough of her
    hye nonny nonny noe.

But gone she is the prettiest lass
    that ever trod on plain.
Whatever hath betide of her
    blame not the shepherd swain,
For why she was her own foe,
    and gave herself the overthrow
By being so frank of her
    hye nonny nonny noe.

Anon

The denial

Nay, pish; nay, phew! nay, faith and will you? Fie!
A gentleman and use me thus! I'll cry.
Nay, God's body, what means this? Nay, fie for shame,
Nay, faith, away! Nay, fie, you are to blame.
Harm! somebody comes! hands off, I pray!
I'll pinch, I'll scratch, I'll spurn, I'll run away.
Nay, faith, you strive in vain, you shall not speed,
You mar my ruff, you hurt my back, I bleed.
Look how the door stands open, somebody sees!
Your buttons scratch, in faith you hurt my knees.
What will men say? Lord, what a coil is here!
You make me sweat, i' faith, here's goodly gear.
Nay, faith, let me entreat you, if you list;
You mar my clothes, you tear my smock; but, had I wist
So much before, I would have shut you out.
Is it a proper thing you go about?
I did not think you would have used me thus,
But now I see I took my aim amiss.
A little thing would make me not be friends:
You've used me well! I hope you'll make amends.
Hold still, I'll wipe your face, you sweat amain:
You have a goodly thing with all your pain.
Alas! how hot am I! What will you drink?
If you go sweating down what will men think?
Remember, sir, how you have used me now;
Doubtless ere long I will be meet with you.
If any man but you had used me so,
Would I have put it up? In faith, sir, no.
Nay, go not yet; stay here and sup with me,
And then at cards we better shall agree.

Anon

A drinker and a wencher

It is not for the love of drink, that I
Carouse so much; but for the company:
No more than it is for the nuptial cranny
That I grimbetilollelize my Jany;
It being her belly, thigh, eyes, arms, mouth, face,
And other such appurtenances, as
    Accompany the integrants, that do it,
    Which so bewitchingly entice me to it.

Anon

Régime de vivre

I rise at eleven, I dine about two,
I get drunk before seven; and the next thing I do,
I send for my whore, when for fear of a clap,
I spend in her hand, and I spew in her lap.
Then we quarrel and scold, 'till I fall fast asleep,
When the bitch, growing bold, to my pocket does creep;
Then slyly she leaves me, and, to revenge the affront,
At once she bereaves me of money and cunt.
If by chance then I wake, hot-headed and drunk,
What a coil do I make for the loss of my punk!
I storm and I roar, and I fall in a rage,
And missing my whore, I bugger my page.
Then, crop-sick all morning, I rail at my men,
And in bed I lie yawning 'till eleven again.

John Wilmot, Earl of Rochester (1647–80)

Of an heroical answer of a great Roman lady to her husband

A grave wise man that had a great rich lady,
Such as perhaps in these days found there may be,
Did think she played him false and more than think,
Save that in wisdom he thereat did wink.
Howbeit one time disposed to sport and play
Thus to his wife he pleasantly did say:
'Since strangers lodge their arrows in thy quiver,
Dear dame, I pray you yet the cause deliver,
If you can tell the cause and not dissemble,
How all our children me so much resemble?'
The lady blushed but yet this answer made:
'Though I have used some traffic in the trade,
And must confess, as you have touched before
My bark was sometimes steered with foreign oar,
    Yet stowed I no man's stuff but first persuaded
    The bottom with your ballast full was laded.'

Sir John Harington (1561–1612)

A ramble in St James's Park

Much wine had passed, with grave discourse
Of who fucks who and who does worse
(Such as you usually do hear
From those who diet at the Bear),
When I, who still take care to see
Drunkenness relieved by lechery,
Went out into St James's Park
To cool my head and fire my heart.
But though St James has the honour on't
'Tis consecrate to prick and cunt.
There by a most incestuous birth
Strange woods spring from the teeming earth,
For they relate how heretofore
When ancient Pict began to whore,
Deluded of his assignation
(Jilting it seems was then in fashion)
Poor pensive lover in this place
Would frig upon his mother's face
Where rows of mandrakes tall did rise
Whose lewd tops fucked the very skies.
Each imitative branch does twine
In some loved fold of Aretine,
And nightly now beneath their shade
Are buggeries, rapes and incests made.
Unto this all-sin-sheltering grove
Whores of the bulk and the alcove,
Great ladies, chambermaids and drudges,
The ragpicker and heiress trudges.
Car-men, divines, great lords and tailors,
Prentices, poets, pimps and jailers,
Footmen, fine fops, do her arrive
And here promiscuously they swive.

Along these hallowed walks it was
That I beheld Corinna pass.
Whoever had been by to see
The proud disdain she cast on me

Through charming eyes, he would have swore
She dropped from heaven that very hour,
Forsaking the divine abode
In scorn of some despairing god.
But mark what creatures women are,
How infinitely vile when fair!

Three knights of the elbow and the slur
With wriggling tails made up to her.

The first was of your Whitehall blades
Near kin to the mother of the Maids,
Graces by whose favour he was able
To bring a friend to the waiters' table,
Where he had heard Sir Edward Sutton
Say how the king loved Banstead mutton;
Since when he'd never be brought to eat
By's good will any other meat.
In this, as well as all the rest,
He ventures to do like the best,
But wanting common sense, the ingredient
In choosing well not least expedient,
Converts abortive imitation
To universal affection.
Thus he not only eats and talks
But feels and smells, sits down and walks,
Nay, looks and lives and loves by rote,
In an old tawdry birthday coat.

The second was a Gray's Inn wit
A great inhabiter of the pit,
Where critic-like he sits and squints,
Steals pocket-handkerchiefs and hints
From neighbour, and the comedy,
To court and pay his landlady.

The third, a lady's eldest son
Within a few years of twenty-one,
Who hopes from his propitious fate
Against he comes to his estate

By these two worthies to be made
A most accomplished tearing blade.

One in a strain 'twixt tune and nonsense
Cries, 'Madam, I have loved you long since.
Permit me your fair hand to kiss' –
When at her mouth her cunt cries 'Yes!'
In short, without much more ado,
Joyful and pleased away she flew
And with these three confounded asses
From park to hackney coach she passes.

So a proud bitch does lead about
Of humble curs the amorous rout
Who most obsequiously to hunt
The savoury scent of salt-swoln cunt.
Some power more patient now relate
The sense of this surprising fate:
Gods that a thing admired by me
Should fall to so much infamy!
Had she picked out to rub her arse on
Some stiff-pricked clown or well-hung parson
Each jet of whose spermatic sluice
Had filled her cunt with wholesome juice,
I the proceeding should have praised
In hope she's quenched a fire I raised.
Such natural freedoms are but just –
There's something generous in mere lust.
But to turn damned abandoned jade
When neither head nor tail persuade –
To be a whore in understanding
A passive pot for fools to spend in!
The devil played booty, sure, with thee
To bring a blot on infamy.

    But why am I, of all mankind,
To so severe a fate designed?
Ungrateful! Why this treachery
To humble, fond, believing me,
Who gave you privilege above

The nice allowances of love?
Did ever I refuse to bear
The meanest part your lust could spare?
When your lewd cunt came spewing home
Drenched with the seed of half the town,
My dram of sperm was supped up after
For the digestive surfeit water.

Full gorgéd at another time
With a vast meal of nasty slime
Which your devouring cunt had drawn
From porters' backs and footmen's brawn,
I was content to serve you up
My bollock-full for your grace cup,
Nor ever thought it an abuse
While you had pleasure for excuse –
You that could make my heart away
For noise and colour, and betray
The secrets of my tender hours
To such knight-errant paramours,
When leaning on your faithless breast
Wrapped in security and rest
Soft kindness all my powers did move
And reason lay dissolved in love!

May stinking vapours choke your womb
Such as the men you dote upon!
May your depraved appetite
That could in whiffling fools delight
Beget such frenzies in your mind
You may go mad for the north wind
And fixing all your hopes upon't
To have him bluster in your cunt,
Turn up your longing arse in the air
And perish in a wild despair!
But cowards shall forget to rant,
Schoolboys to frig, old whores to paint;
The Jesuits' fraternity
Shall leave the use of buggery;
Crab-louse, inspired with grace divine,

From earthly cod to heaven shall climb;
Physicians shall believe in Jesus
And disobedience cease to please us
Ere I desist with all my power
To plague this woman and undo her.
But my revenge will best be timed
When she is married that is limed.
In that most lamentable state
I'll make her feel my scorn and hate,
Pelt her with scandals, truth or lies,
And her poor cur with jealousies
Till I have torn him from her breech
While she whines like a dog-drawn bitch,
Loathed and despised, kicked out of the town
Into some dirty hole alone
To chew the cud of misery
And know she owes it all to me.

And may no woman better thrive
That dares profane the cunt I swive!

John Wilmot, Earl of Rochester (1647–80)

Nell Gwynne

Hard by Pall Mall lives a wench called Nell
   King Charles the Second he kept her
She hath got a trick to handle his prick,
   But never lays hands on his sceptre.
All matters of state from her soul she does hate,
   And leaves to the politic bitches.
The whore's in the right, for 'tis her delight
   To be scratching just where it itches

Anon

Molly

Molly owned a shellfish stall
She'd serve you in a twinkle
And if you didn't know the way,
She'd soon fish out your winkle.

Anon

A modern young woman from France

A modern young woman from France
Went out to a birth control dance.
   She took all her pessaries
   And other accessories,
And didn't leave babies to chance.

Anon

BELL ENDS
AND BEAVERS

'From grievous disappointments
To jubilant surprises'

Anon

Figs

The proper way to eat a fig, in society,
Is to split it in four, holding it by the stump,
And open it, so that it is a glittering, rosy, moist, honied, heavy-
petalled four-petalled flower.

Then you throw away the skin
Which is just like a four-sepalled calyx,
After you have taken off the blossom with your lips.

But the vulgar way
Is just to put your mouth to the crack, and take out the flesh in
one bite.

Every fruit has its secret.

The fig is a very secretive fruit.
As you see it standing growing, you feel at once it is symbolic:
And it seems male.
But when you come to know it better, you agree with the
Romans, it is female.

The Italians vulgarly say, it stands for the female part; the fig-fruit:
The fissure, the yoni,
The wonderful moist conductivity towards the centre.

Involved,
Inturned,
The flowering all inward and womb-fibrilled;
And but one orifice.

The fig, the horse-shoe, the squash-blossom.
Symbols.

There was a flower that flowered inward, womb-ward;
Now there is a fruit like a ripe womb.

It was always a secret.
That's how it should be, the female should always be secret.

There never was any standing aloft and unfolded on a bough
Like other flowers, in a revelation of petals;
Silver-pink peach, venetian green glass of medlars and sorb-apples,
Shallow wine-cups on short, bulging stems
Openly pledging heaven:
Here's to the thorn in flower! Here is to Utterance!
The brave, adventurous rosaceæ.

Folded upon itself, and secret unutterable,
And milky-sapped, sap that curdles milk and makes *ricotta*,
Sap that smells strange on your fingers, that even goats won't taste
it;
Folded upon itself, enclosed like any Mohammedan woman,
Its nakedness all within-walls, its flowering forever unseen,
One small way of access only, and this close-curtained from the
light;
Fig, fruit of the female mystery, convert and inward,
Mediterranean fruit, with your covert nakedness,
Where everything happens invisible, flowering and fertilisation,
and fruiting
In the inwardness of your you, that eye will never see
Till it's finished, and you're over-ripe, and you burst to give up
your ghost.

Till the drop of ripeness exudes,
And the year is over.

And then the fig has kept her secret long enough.
So it explodes, and you see through the fissure the scarlet.
And the fig is finished, the year is over.

That's how the fig dies, showing her crimson through the purple
slit
Like a wound, the exposure of her secret, on the open day.
Like a prostitute, the bursten fig, making a show of her secret.

That's how women die too.

The year is fallen over-ripe,
The year of our women.
The year of our women is fallen over-ripe.
The secret is laid bare.
And rottenness soon sets in.
The year of our women is fallen over-ripe.

When Eve once knew *in her mind* that she was naked
She quickly sewed fig-leaves, and sewed the same for the man.
She'd been naked all her days before,
But till then, till that apple of knowledge, she hadn't had the fact
on her mind.

She got the fact on her mind, and quickly sewed fig-leaves.
And women have been sewing ever since.
But now they stitch to adorn the bursten fig, not to cover it.
They have their nakedness more than ever on their mind,
And they won't let us forget it.

Now, the secret
Becomes an affirmation through moist, scarlet lips
That laugh at the Lord's indignation.

What then, good Lord! cry the women.
We have kept our secret long enough.
We are a ripe fig.
Let us burst into affirmation.

They forget, ripe figs won't keep.
Ripe figs won't keep.

Honey-white figs of the north, black figs with scarlet inside, of
the south.
Ripe figs won't keep, won't keep in any clime.
What then, when women the world over have all bursten into
self-assertion?
And bursten figs won't keep?

D. H. Lawrence (1885–1930)

133

The author to his wife, of a woman's eloquence

My Mall, I mark that when you mean to prove me
To buy a velvet gown, or some rich border,
Thou callst me good sweet heart, thou swearst to love me,
Thy locks, thy lips, thy looks, speak all in order,
Thou thinks, and right thou thinks, that these do move me,
That all these severally thy suit do further:
    But shall I tell thee what most thy suit advances?
    Thy fair smooth words? no, no, thy fair smooth haunches.

Sir John Harington (1561–1612)

Um Chukka Willy

Um Chuckka Willy
of Coconut Grove
was a mean motherfucker
you could tell by his clothes.
Black leather jacket
and hairy arse,
between his balls was a patch of grass,
led a hundred women
through a hole in the wall,
swore to the devil
he'd fuck 'em all.
At ninety-nine
he had to stop,
the friction on his balls
was about to pop.
Went to the doctor
and the doctor said,
'Um Chukka Willy
your balls are dead.'

Anon

I have a noble cockerel

I have a noble cockerel
Whose crowing starts my day:
He makes me get up early
My morning prayer to say.

I have a noble cockerel
Of lofty pedigree:
His comb is of red coral,
His tail jet-black to see.

I have a noble cockerel;
He comes of gentle kind:
His comb is of red coral,
His tail is of Ind.

His legs are all of azure,
Graceful, soft, and slim:
His spurs are silver white
Deep to the root of him.

His eyes are of crystal,
Sweetly set in amber;
And every night he perches
In my lady's chamber.

Anon
(Trans. Brian Stone)

Epigram XXXIII

If from the baths you hear a round of applause,
Maron's great prick is bound to be the cause.

Martial (c. AD 40–c. 104)
(Trans. James Michie)

A beehive

My mistress in a hive of bees,
In yonder flowery garden.
They come to her with laden thighs,
To ease them of their burden.
As under the beehive lies the wax,
And under the wax is honey,
So under her waist her belly is placed,
And under that, her cunny.

Anon

One writing against his prick

Base metal hanger by your master's thigh!
Eternal shame to all Prick's heraldry,
Hide thy despisèd head and do not dare
To peep, no not so much as take the air
But through a button hole, but pine and die
Confined within the codpiece monastery.
The little childish boy that hardly knows
The way through which his urine flows
Touched by my mistress her magnetic hand
His little needle presently will stand.
Did she not raise thy drooping head on high
As it lay nodding on her wanton thigh?
Did she not clap her legs about my back
Her port-hole open? Damned Prick what is't you lack?
Henceforth stand stiff and gain your credit lost
Or I'll ne'er draw thee but against a post.

Anon (c. 1680)

Upon the nipples of Julia's breast

Have you beheld (with much delight)
A red rose peeping through a white?
Or else a cherry (double graced)
Within a lily? Centre placed?
Or ever marked the pretty beam,
A strawberry shows, half drowned in cream?
Or seen rich rubies blushing through
A pure smooth pearl, and orient too?
So like to this, nay all the rest,
Is each neat niplet of her breast.

Robert Herrick (1591–1674)

Epigrams on Priapus

Though I be wooden Priapus (as thou seeest),
With wooden sickle and a prickle of wood,
Yet will I seize thee, Girl! and hold thee seized
And This, however gross, withouten fraud
Stiffer than Lyre-string or than twisted rope
I'll thrust and bury to thy seventh rib.

Why laugh such laughter, O most silly maid?
My form Praxiteles nor Scopas hewed:
To me no Phidian handwork finish gave;

But me a bailiff hacked from shapeless log,
And quoth my maker, 'Thou Priapus be!'
Yet on me gazing forthright gigglest thou
And holdest funny matter to deride
The pillar perking from the groin of me.

Anon (c. 1889)

from The priapean corpus, ix

To your question: why are my private parts
not covered? My reply is: deities don't conceal
their weapons. The king of the sky
brandishes his thunderbolt openly,
the seas' lord includes the trident
among his regalia.
Mars won't hide his sword, his symbol of power,
the spear of Pallas is not tucked within
the warm folds of her cloak.
Does it shame Phoebus to carry his golden arrows?
Does Diana blush to flex her bow?
Does Hercules conceal his knotty cudgel,
Mercury his wand? Who's seen Bacchus
drape his graceful thyrsus,
Cupid dim his lighted torch?
Don't rebuke me, then, for exposing my phallus.
With it I'm armed,
without it I'm nothing.

Anon
(Trans: Eugene O'Connor)

The tenement

If any man do want a house,
Be he prince, baronet or squire,
Or peasant, hardly worth a louse,
   I can fit his desire.

I have a tenement the which
I'm sure can fit them all;
'Tis seated near a stinking ditch,
   Some call it Cunny Hall.

It stands close by Cunny Alley
At foot of Belly Hill.
Thsi house is freely to be let
   To whom soever will.

For term of life or years or days
I'll let this pleasant bower,
Nay, rather than a tenant want,
   I'll let it for an hour.

About it grows a lofty wood
Will save you from the sun;
Well watered 'tis, for throughout
   A pleasant stream doth run.

If hot, you there may cool yourself,
If cool, you'll there find heat;
For greatest 'tis not too little
   For least 'tis not too great.

I must confess my house is dark,
Be it by night or day,
But when you're once but got therein
   You'll never lose your way.

And when you're in go boldy on
As fast as e'er you can,
For if you go to the end thereof
    You go where ne'er did man.

But though my house be deep and dark,
'T has many a man made merry,
And in't much liquor has been spent
    More precious than the sherry.

Thus if you like my Cunny Hall
Your house-room shall be good,
For such a temper as you find
    Burns neither cole nor wood,

For if it rain or freeze or snow –
To speak I dare be bold –
If you keep your nose within the door
    You ne'er shall feel the cold.

But I must convenant with him
That takes this house of mine,
Whether it be for term of life
    Or else for shorter time.

See that you dress it twice a day
And rub it round about,
And if you do dislike of this
    I'll seek a new tenant out.

Anon (c. 1671)

Epigram XXXIV

Lesbia, why are your amours
Always conducted behind open, unguarded doors?
Why do you get more excitement out of a voyeur than a lover?
Why is pleasure no pleasure when it's under cover?
Whores use a curtain, a bolt or a porter
To bar the public – you won't find many chinks in the red-light
quarter.
Ask Chione or Ias how to behave:
Even the cheapest tart conceals her business inside a monumental
grave.
If I seem too hard on you, remember my objection
Is not to fornication but detection.

Martial (c. AD 40–c. 104)
(Trans. James Michie)

Terminology

Those parts that attract male depravity
Are fashioned with wondrous care,
And what looks like a simple small cavity
Is really an elaborate affair.

There's the vulva, vagina, perineum,
The clitoris and much more besides;
Small beauties if you know how to use them,
For yourself and your girlfriend or bride.

So it's a pity the male race does chatter
About the things to which I have referred,
And uses for this delicate matter
A short, unappealing little word.

Anon

A riddle

Come, pretty nymph, fain would I know
What thing it is that breeds delight,
That strives to stand, and cannot go,
And feeds the mouth that cannot bite.

It is a kind of pleasing thing,
A pricking and a piercing sting.
It is Venus' wanton wand.
It hath no legs, and yet can stand.
A bachelor's button thoroughly ripe,
The kindest new tobacco-pipe.

It is the pen that Helen took
To write in her two-leavèd book.
It's a prick-shaft of Cupid's cut,
Yet some do shoot it at a butt.
And every wench by her good will
Would keep it in her quiver still.
The fairest yet that ever had life
For love of this became a wife.

Anon (c. 1600)

Nine inch will please a lady

Come rede[1] me, dame, come tell me, dame,
    My dame, come tell me truly,
What length o' graith,[2] when weel ca'd hame[3]
    Will serve a woman duly?
The carlin[4] clew her wanton tail,
    Her wanton tail sae ready;
I learnt a sang in Annandale,
    Nine inch will please a lady.

But for a countrie cunt like mine,
    In sooth we're nae sae tentle;
We'll take twa thumb-bread to the nine,
    And that's a sonsie[5] pintle.[6]
O leeze me[7] on my Charlie lad!
    I'll ne'er forget my Charlie;
Twa roarin handfu' and a daud,[8]
    He nidg't it in fu'[9] rarely.

But weary fa' the laithern doup,[10]
    And may it ne'er ken thrivin';
It's no the length that gars me loup,[11]
    But it's the double drivin'.
Come nidge me Tam, come nodge me Tam,
    Come nidge me o'er the nyvel;[12]
Come loose and lug your batterin' ram,
    And thrash him at my gyvel.

Robert Burns (1759–96)

[1] rede = teach
[2] graith = instrument
[3] ca'd hame = hit home
[4] carlin = crone
[5] sonsie = fat, lively
[6] pintle = penis
[7] leeze me = I was pleased
[8] daud = large surplus
[9] fu' = full
[10] laithern doup = sweaty buttocks
[11] gars me loup = makes me jump
[12] nyvel = navel

In winter, in my room

In winter, in my room,
I came upon a worm,
Pink, lank, and warm.
But as he was a worm
And worms presume,
Not quite with him at home –
Secured him by a string
To something neighbouring,
And went along.

A trifle afterward
A thing occurred,
I'd not believe it if I heard –
But state with creeping blood;
A snake, with mottles rare,
Surveyed my chamber floor,
In feature as the worm before,
But ringed with power.
The very string
With which I tied him, too,
When he was mean and new,
That string was there.

I shrank – 'how fair you are!'
Propitiation's claw –
'Afraid,' he hissed,
'Of me?'
'No cordiality?'
He fathomed me.
Then, to a rhythm slim
Secreted in his form,
As patterns swim,
Projected him.

That time I flew,
Both eyes his way,
Lest he pursue –
Nor ever ceased to run,
Till, in a distant town,
Towns on from mine –

I sat me down;
This was a dream.

Emily Dickinson
(1830–86)

Stand, stately Tavie

Stand, stately Tavie, out of the codpiece rise,
And dig a grave between thy mistress' thighs,
Swift stand, then stab 'till she replies,
Then gently weep, and after weeping, die.
Stand, Tavie, and gain thy credit lost,
Or by this hand I'll never draw thee, but against a post.

Anon

The hairy prospect

Once on a time the Sire of evil,
In plainer English called the devil,
Some new experiment to try
At Chloe cast a roguish eye;
But she who all his arts defied,
Pulled up and showed her sex's pride:
A thing all shagged about with hair,
So much it made old Satan stare,
Who frightened at the grim display,
Takes to his heels and runs away.

Attributed to Thomas Rowlandson
(1756–1827)

Busts and bosoms have I known

Busts and bosoms have I known
　　Of various shapes and sizes
From grievous disappointments
　　To jubilant surprises.

Anon

My friend Billy

My friend Billy's got a ten foot willy,
he showed it to the girl next door.
She thought it was a snake
so she hit it with a rake,
and now it's only four foot four.

Anon

There was a young man of Devizes

There was a young man of Devizes
Whose testes were two different
sizes.
   The one was so small
   It was no ball at all;
But the other one won several prizes.

Anon

There once was a young man of Ghent

There once was a young man of Ghent
Whose tool was so long that it bent.
   To save himself trouble
   He put it in double,
And instead of coming, he went.

Anon

DAMP SQUIBS
AND OTHER
DISAPPOINTMENTS

'Away he went when all was spent,
whereat she was offended'

Anon

On a bashful shepherd

Young Clovis by a happy chance,
His loved Ephelia spied,
In such a place, as might advance
His courage, and abate her pride:
With eyes that might have told his suit,
Although his bashful tongue was mute,
Upon her gazed he,
But the coy nymph, though in surprise,
Upon the ground fixing her eyes,
The language would not see.

With gentle grasps he wooed her hand,
And sighed in seeming pain,
But this she would not understand,
His sighs were all in vain:
Then change of blushes next he tried,
And gave his hand freedom to slide
Upon her panting breast;
Finding she did not this control,
Unto her lips he gently stole,
And bid her guess the rest.

She blushed, and turned her head aside,
And so much anger feigned,
That the poor shepherd almost died,
And she no breath retained:
Her killing frown so chilled his blood,
He like a senseless statue stood,
Nor further durst he woo,
And though his blessing was so near,
Checked by his modesty and fear,
He faintly let it go.

'Ephelia'

To his mistress, objecting to him neither toying or talking

You say I love not, 'cause I do not play
Still with your curls, and kiss the time away.
You blame me, too, because I can't devise
Some sport, to please those babies in your eyes; –
By Love's religion, I must here confess it,
The most I love, when I the least express it.
Small griefs find tongues; full casks are ever found
To give, if any, yet but little sound.
Deep waters noiseless are; and this we know,
That chiding streams betray small depth below.
So when love speechless is, she doth express
A depth in love, and that depth bottomless.
Now, since my love is tongueless, know me such,
Who speak but little, 'cause I love so much.

Robert Herrick (1591–1674)

She lay all naked

She lay all naked in her bed,
    And I myself lay by;
No veil but curtains about her spread,
    No covering but I:
Her head upon her shoulders seeks
    To hang in careless wise,
And full of blushes was her cheeks,
    And of wishes were her eyes.

Her blood still fresh into her face,
    As on a message came,
To say that in another place
    It meant another game;
Her cherry lip moist, plump, and fair,
    Millions of kisses crown,
Which ripe and uncropped dangled there,
    And weigh the branches down.

Her breasts, that welled so plump and high
    Bred pleasant pain in me,
For all the world I do defy
    The like felicity;
Her thighs and belly, soft and fair,
    To me were only shown:
To have seen such meat, and not to have eat,
    Would have angered any stone.

Her knees lay upward gently bent,
    And all lay hollow under,
As if on easy terms, they meant
    To fall unforced asunder;
Just so the Cyprian Queen did lie,
    Expecting in her bower;
When too long stay had kept the boy
    Beyond his promised hour.

'Dull clown,' quoth she, 'why dost delay
    Such proffered bliss to take?
Canst thou find out no other way
    Similitudes to make?'
Mad with delight I thundering
    Throw my arms about her,
But pox upon't 'twas but a dream.
    And so I lay without her.

Anon (17th c.)

The imperfect enjoyment

Naked she lay, clasped in my longing arms,
I filled with love, and she all over charms,
Both equally inspired with eager fire,
Melting through kindness, flaming in desire.
With arms, lips, legs close clinging to embrace,
She clips me to her breast, and sucks me to her face.
The nimble tongue (love's lesser lightning) played
Within my mouth, and to my thoughts conveyed
Swift orders that I should prepare to throw
The all-dissolving thunderbolt below.
My fluttering soul, sprung with the pointed kiss,
Hangs hovering over her balmy limbs of bliss.
But whilst her busy hand would guide that part
Which should convey my soul up to her heart,
In liquid raptness I dissolve all over,
Melting in love, such joys never felt before.
A touch from any part of her had done it,
Her hand, her foot, her very looks had charms upon it.
Smiling, she chides in a soft murmuring noise,
And sighs to feel the too-too hasty joys;
When with a thousand kisses, wand'ring o'er
My panting breast – and is there then no more?
She cries: All this to love and raptures due,
Must we not pay a debt to pleasure too?

But I the most forlorn, lost man alive
To show my wished obedience vainly strive.
I sigh, alas, and kiss, but cannot drive.
Eager desires confound my first intent,
Succeeding shame does more success prevent,
And rage at last confirms me impotent.
Even her fair hands which might bid heat return
To frozen age, and make cold hermits burn,
Applied to my dead cinder warms no more
Than fire to ashes could past flames restore.
Trembling, confused, despairing, limber, dry,
A wishing, weak, unmoving lump I lie.

This dart of love, whose piercing point oft tried
With virgin blood, a hundred maids has dyed,
Which nature still directed with such art
That it, through every port, reached every heart.
Stiffly resolved, turned careless I invade,
Where it essayed, nor ought its fury stayed,
Where ever it pierced, entrance it found or made,
Now languid lies, in this unhappy hour,
Shrunk up and sapless, like a withered flower.

Thou treacherous, base, deserter of my flame,
False to my passion, fatal to my fame,
By what mistaken magic dost thou prove
So true to lewdness, so untrue to love?
What oyster, cinder, beggar, common whore,
Didst thou e'er fail in all thy life before?
When vice, disease, and scandal led the way
With what officious haste didst thou obey?
Like a rude-roaring Hector in the streets
That scuffles, cuffs, and ruffles all he meets;
But if his King or country claim his aid
The rascal villain shrinks and hides his head;
Even so is thy brutal valour displayed,
Breaks every stews, does each small crack invade,
But if great love the onset does command,
Base recreant to thy Prince, thou dost not stand.
Worst part of me and henceforth hated most,
Through all the town the common rubbing-post,
On whom each wretch relieves her lustful want,
As hogs on goats do rub themselves and grunt,
May'st thou to ravenous shankers be a prey,
Or in consuming weepings waste away;
May stranguries and stone thy days attend.
May'st thou not piss who did'st so much offend
When all my joys did on false thee depend.
And may ten thousand abler men agree
To do the wronged Corinna right for thee.

John Wilmot, Earl of Rochester (1647–80)

The sick rose

O Rose, thou art sick!
The invisible worm
That flies in the night,
In the howling storm

Has found out thy bed
Of crimson joy:
And his dark secret love
Does thy life destroy.

William Blake
(1757–1827)

Walking in a meadow green

(Song)

Walking in a meadow green
   fair flowers for to gather,
where primrose ranks did stand on banks
   to welcome comers thither,
I heard a voice which made a noise,
   which caused me to attend it,
I heard a lass say to a lad
   'Once more, and none can mend it.'

They lay so close together,
   they made me much to wonder;
I know not which was whether
   until I saw her under.
Then off he came, and blushed for shame
   so soon that he had end it;
yet still she lies, and to him cries,
   'Once more, and none can mend it.'

His looks were dull and very sad,
   his courage she had tamed;
she bade him play the lusty lad
   or else he quite was shamed;
'then stiffly thrust, he hit me just,
   fear not, but freely spend it,
and play about at in and out;
   once more, and none can mend it.'

And then he thought to enter her,
   thinking the fit was on him;
but when he came to enter her,
   the point turned back upon him.
Yet she said, 'stay! go not away
   although the point he bended!
but to it again, and hit the vaine!
   once more, and none can mend it.'

Then in her arms, she did him fold,
    and oftentimes she kissed him;
yet still his courage was but cold
    for all the good she wished him;
yet with her hand she made it stand
    so stiff she could not bend it,
and then anon she cries 'come on
    once more, and none can mend it!'

'Adieu, adieu, sweet heart,' quoth he,
    'for in faith I must be gone.'
'Nay, then you do me wrong,' quoth she,
    'to leave me thus alone.'
Away he went when all was spent,
    whereat she was offended;
Like a Trojan true she made a vow
    she would have one should mend it.

Anon (c. 1660)

The women's complaint to Venus

How happy were good English faces
   Till Monsieur from France
   Taught pego a dance
To the tune of old Sodom's embraces.

But now we are quite out of fashion:
   Poor whores may be nuns
   Since men turn their guns
And vent on each other their passion.

In the reign of good Charles the Second
   Full many a jade
   A lady was made
And the issue right noble was reckoned,

But now we find to our sorrow
   We are overrun
   By sparks of the bum
And peers of the land of Gomorrah.

The beaux too, whom most we relied on,
   At night make a punk
   Of him that's first drunk
Though unfit for the sport as John Dryden.

The soldiers, whom next we put trust in,
   No widow can tame
   Or virgin reclaim
But at the wrong place will be thrusting.

Fair Venus, thou goddess of beauty,
   Receive our complaint,
   Make Rigby recant
And the soldiers henceforth do their duty.

Anon (c. 1698)

I, being born a woman and distressed

I, being born a woman and distressed
By all the needs and notions of my kind,
Am urged by your propinquity to find
Your person fair, and feel a certain zest
To bear your body's weight upon my breast:
So subtly is the fume of life designed,
To clarify the pulse and cloud the mind,
And leave me once again undone, possessed.
Think not for this, however, the poor treason
Of my stout blood against my staggering brain,
I shall remember you with love, or season
My scorn with pity, – let me make it plain:
I find this frenzy insufficient reason
For conversation when we meet again.

Edna St Vincent Millay (1892–1950)

The vine

I dreamed this mortal part of mine
Was metamorphosed to a vine;
Which crawling one and every way,
Enthralled my dainty Lucia.
Me thought, her long small legs and thighs
I with my tendrils did surprise;
Her belly, buttocks, and her waist
By now soft nervelets were embraced
About her head I writhing hung,
And with rich clusters (hid among
The leaves) her temples I behung
So that my Lucia seemed to me
Young Bacchus ravished by his tree.
My curls about her neck did crawl,
And arms and hands they did enthral:
So that she could not freely stir,
All parts there made one prisoner.
But when I crept with leaves to hide
Those parts, which maids keep unespied,
Such fleeting pleasures there I took,
That with the fancy I awoke;
And found (Ah me!) this flesh of mine
More like a stock, than like a vine.

Robert Herrick (1591–1674)

Elegies, III

Either she was foul, or her attire was bad,
Or she was not the wench I wished to have had.
Idly I lay with her, as if I loved not,
And like a burthen grieved the bed that moved not.
Though both of us performed our true intent,
Yet could I not cast anchor where I meant.
She on my neck her ivory arms did throw,
Her arms far whiter than the Scythian snow.
And eagerly she kissed me with her tongue,
And under mine her wanton thigh she flung.
Yea, and she soothed me up, and called me sir,
And used all speech that might provoke, and stir.
Yet like as if cold hemlock I had drunk,
It mocked me, hung down the head, and sunk.
Like a dull cipher, or rude block I lay:
Or shade or body was I, who can say?
What will my age do, age I cannot shun,
When in my prime my force is spent and done?
I blush, that being youthful, hot and lusty,
I prove neither youth nor man, but old and rusty. . . .

Worthy she was to move both gods and men,
But neither was I man, nor lived then.
Can deaf ear take delight when Phaemius sings?
Or Thamiras in curious painted things?
What sweet thought is there but I had the same?
And one gave place still as another came.
Yet notwithstanding like one dead it lay,
Drooping more than a rose pulled yesterday.
Now when he should not jet, he bolts upright,
And craves his task, and seeks to be at fight.
Lie down with shame, and see thou stir no more,
Seeing thou would deceive me as before.
Thou cozenest me: by thee surprised am I,
And bid sore loss with endless infamy.
Nay more, the wench did not disdain a whit,
To take it in her hand and play with it.

But when she saw it would by no means stand,
But still dropped down, regarding not her hand,
'Why mockest though me?' she cried, 'or, being ill,
Who bade thee lie down here against thy will?
Either thou art witched with blood of frogs new dead
Or jaded you came from some other's bed.'
With that, her loose gown on, from me she cast her.
In skipping out her naked feet much graced her.
And lest her maid should know of this disgrace,
To cover it, spilt water on the place.

Ovid (43 BC–AD 18)
(Trans. Christopher Marlowe)

from The disappointment

VII
He saw how at her length she lay.
He saw her rising bosom bare,
Her loose, thin robes, through which appear
A shape designed for love and play,
Abandoned by her pride and shame.
She does her softest joys dispense,
Offering her virgin-innocence
A victim to love's sacred flame,
While the o'er-ravished shepherd lies
Unable to perform the sacrifice.

VIII
Ready to taste a thousand joys,
The too transported, hapless swain
Found the vast pleasure turned to pain –
Pleasure which too much love destroys:
The willing garments by he laid,
And heaven all opened to his view.
Mad to possess, himself he threw
On the defenceless, lovely maid.
But oh, what envying gods conspire
To snatch his power, yet leave him the desire!

IX
Nature's support (without whose aid
She can no human being give)
Itself now wants the art to live;
Faintness its slackened nerves invade.
In vain th'enraged youth essayed
To call its fleeting vigour back,
No motion 'twill from motion take.
Excess of love is Love betrayed.
In vain he toils, in vain commands –
Insensible falls weeping in his hands.

X

In this so amorous, cruel strife
Where love and fate were too severe
The poor Lysander in despair
Renounced his reason with his life.
Now all the brisk and active fire
That should the nobler part inflame
Served to increase his rage and shame
And left no spark for new desire:
Not all her naked charms could move
Or calm that rage that had debauched his love

XI

Cloris returning from the trance
Which love and soft desire had bred,
Her timorous hand she gently laid
(Or guided by desire or chance)
Upon that fabulous priapus,
That potent god, as poets feign –
But never did young shepherdess
Gathering of fern upon the plain
More nimbly draw her fingers back
Finding beneath the verdant leaves a snake:

XII

Than Cloris her fair hand withdrew,
Finding that god of her desires
Disarmed of all his awful fires
And cold as flowers bathed in the morning dew.
Who can the nymph's confusion guess?
The blood forsook the hinder place
And strewed with blushes all her face,
Which both disdain and shame expressed;
And from Lysander's arms she fled,
Leaving him fainting on the gloomy bed.

XIII

Like lightning through the groves she hies,
Or Daphne from the Delphic god;
No print upon the grassy road
She leaves, t'instruct pursuing eyes.
The wind that wantoned in her hair
And with her ruffled garments played
Discovered in the flying maid
All that the gods e'er made, if fair.
So Venus, when her love was slain,
With fear and haste flew o'er that fatal plain.

XIV

The nymph's resentments none but I
Can well imagine or condole.
But none can guess Lysander's soul
But those who swayed his destiny.
His silent griefs swell up to storms,
And not one god his fury spares;
He cursed his birth, his fate, his stars –
But more the shepherdess's charms,
Whose soft, bewitching influence
Had damned him to the hell of impotence.

Aphra Behn (1640–89)

Here lies the body

Here lies the body
of dear old Dick
who went through life
with a twisted prick.

All his life
was a lifelong hunt
looking for the girl
with the twisted cunt.

When he found one
he dropped down dead,
for the one he found
had a left-hand thread.

Anon

There was a young actress called Sue

There was a young actress called Sue
Who said, as the bishop withdrew,
   'The vicar is quicker,
   And slicker and thicker,
And five inches longer than you.'

Anon

A lonely young man from Norway

A lonely young man from Norway
Tried to masturbate whilst in a sleigh.
   But the howling wind froze
   His balls to his nose
And all he produced was frappé.

Anon

A remarkable tribe are the Sweenies

A remarkable tribe are the Sweenies,
Renowned for the length of their penes.
   The hair on their balls,
    Sweeps the floors of their halls,
But they don't care for women, the meanies.

Anon

There was a young man from Berlin

There was a young man from Berlin
Whose tool was the size of a pin.
   Said his girl with a laugh
    As she fondled his shaft,
'Well, this won't be much of a sin.'

Anon

An unfortunate pirate called Bates

An unfortunate pirate called Bates
Liked to do the fandango on skates.
　　But he fell on his cutlass
　　Which rendered him nutless
And practically useless on dates.

Anon

A beautiful lass from Saigon

A beautiful lass from Saigon
Had a clitoris twelve inches long.
　　This embarrassed her lover
　　Who was pained to discover
She expected no less of his dong.

Anon

YEARNING

'Would that my hands were there'
Carmina Burana

from Carmina Burana

Innocent breasts, when I have looked upon them,
    Would that my hands were there,
How have I craved, and dreaming thus upon them,
    Love wakened from despair.
        Beauty on her lips flaming,
        Rose red with her shaming,
        And I with passion burning
        And with my whole heart yearning
For her mouth, her mouth, her mouth,
That on her beauty I might slake my drouth.

Anon (c. 13th century)
(Trans. Helen Waddell)

The vision

Sitting alone (as one forsook)
Close by a silver-shedding brook;
With hands held up to love, I wept;
And after sorrows spent, I slept.
Then in a vision I did see
A glorious form appear to me:
A virgin's face she had; her dress
Was like a sprightly Spartaness.
A silver bow with green silk strung
Down from her comely shoulders hung;
And as she stood, the wanton air
Dangled the ringlets of her hair.
Her legs were such Diana shows,
When tucked up she a-hunting goes;
With buskins shortened to descry
The happy dawning of her thigh:
Which when I saw, I made access
To kiss that tempting nakedness.
But she forbade me, with a wand
Of myrtle she had in her hand;
And chiding me, said, hence, remove,
Herrick, thou art too coarse to love.

Robert Herrick (1591–1674)

In a gondola

The moth's kiss, first!
Kiss me as if you made believe
You were not sure, this eve,
How my face, your flower, had pursed
Its petals up; so, here and there
You brush it, till I grow aware
Who wants me, and wide ope I burst.

The bee's kiss, now!
Kiss me as if you entered gay
My heart at some noonday,
A bud that dares not disallow
The claim, so all is rendered up,
And passively its shattered cup
Over your head to sleep I bow.

Robert Browning (1812–89)

Faded leaves

Longing

Come to me in my dreams, and then
By day I shall be well again.
For so the night will more than pay
The hopeless longing of the day.

Come, as thou camest a thousand times,
A messenger from radiant climes,
And smile on thy new world, and be
As kind to others as to me.

Or, as thou never camest in sooth,
Come now, and let me dream it truth.
And part my hair, and kiss my brow,
And say: *My love! why sufferest thou?*

Come to me in my dreams, and then
By day I shall be well again.
For so the night will more than pay
The hopeless longing of the day.

Matthew Arnold (1822–88)

Echo

Come to me in the silence of the night;
   Come in the speaking silence of a dream;
Come with soft rounded cheeks and eyes as bright
   As sunlight on a stream;
     Come back in tears,
O memory, hope, love of finished years.

Oh dream how sweet, too sweet, too bitter sweet,
   Whose wakening should have been in Paradise,
Where souls brimfull of love abide and meet;
   Where thirsting longing eyes
     Watch the slow door
That opening, letting in, lets out no more.

Yet come to me in dreams, that I may live
   My very life again tho' cold in death:
Come back to me in dreams, that I may give
   Pulse for pulse, breath for breath:
     Speak low, lean low,
As long ago, my love, how long ago.

Christina Rossetti (1830–94)

The Eve of St Agnes

St Agnes' Eve – Ah, bitter chill it was!
The owl, for all his feathers, was a-cold;
The hare limp'd trembling through the frozen grass,
And silent was the flock in woolly fold:
Numb were the Beadsman's fingers while he told
His rosary, and while his frosted breath,
Like pious incense from a censer old,
Seem'd taking flight for heaven, without a death,
Past the sweet Virgin's picture, while his prayer he saith.

His prayer he saith, this patient, holy man:
Then takes his lamp, and riseth from his knees,
And back returneth, meagre, barefoot, wan,
Along the chapel aisle by slow degrees:
The sculptured dead, on each side, seem to freeze,
Emprison'd in black, purgatorial rails:
Knights, ladies, praying in dumb orat'ries,
He passeth by, and his weak spirit fails
To think how they may ache in icy hoods and mails.

Northward he turneth through a little door,
And scarce three steps, ere Music's golden tongue
Flatter'd to tears this aged man and poor.
But no – already had his death-bell rung;
The joys of all his life were said and sung:
His was harsh penance on St Agnes' Eve:
Another way he went, and soon among
Rough ashes sat he for his soul's reprieve,
And all night kept awake, for sinners' sake to grieve.

That ancient Beadsman heard the prelude soft;
And so it chanced, for many a door was wide,
From hurry to and fro. Soon, up aloft,
The silver, snarling trumpets 'gan to chide:
The level chambers, ready with their pride,
Were glowing to receive a thousand guests:
The carvèd angels, ever eager-eyed,
Stared, where upon their heads the cornice rests,
With hair blown back, and wings put crosswise on their breasts.

At length burst in the argent revelry,
With plume, tiara, and all rich array,
Numerous as shadows haunting fairly,
The brain new-stuffed, in youth, with triumphs gay
Of old romance. These let us wish away,
And turn, sole-thoughted, to one Lady there,
Whose heart had brooded, all that wintry day,
On love, and winged St Agnes' saintly care,
As she had heard old dames full many times declare.

They told her how, upon St Agnes' Eve,
Young virgins might have visions of delight,
And soft adorings from their loves receive,
Upon the honeyed middle of the night,
If ceremonies due they did aright;
As, supperless to bed they must retire,
And couch supine their beauties, lily white;
Nor look behind, nor sideways, but require
Of Heaven with upward eyes for all that they desire.

Full of this whim was thoughtful Madeline:
The music, yearning like a God in pain,
She scarcely heard: her maiden eyes divine,
Fixed on the floor, saw many a sweeping train
Pass by – she heeded not at all: in vain
Came many a tiptoe, amorous cavalier,
And back retired; not cooled by high disdain,
But she saw not: her heart was otherwhere,
She sighed for Agnes' dreams, the sweetest of the year.

She danced along with vague, regardless eyes,
  Anxious her lips, her breathing quick and short:
  The hallowed hour was near at hand: she sighs
  Amid the timbrels, and the thronged resort
  Of whisperers in anger, or in sport;
  'Mid looks of love, defiance, hate, and scorn,
  Hoodwinked with faery fancy; all amort,
  Save to St Agnes and her lambs unshorn,
And all the bliss to be before to-morrow morn.

  So, purposing each moment to retire,
  She lingered still. Meantime, across the moors
  Had come young Porphyro, with heart on fire
  For Madeline. Beside the portal doors,
  Buttressed from moonlight, stands he, and implores
  All saints to give him sight of Madeline,
  But for one moment in the tedious hours,
  That he might gaze and worship all unseen;
Perchance speak, kneel, touch, kiss – in sooth such things have
been.

  He ventures in: let no buzzed whisper tell,
  All eyes be muffled, or a hundred swords
  Will storm his heart, Love's feverous citadel:
  For him, those chambers held barbarian hordes,
  Hyena foemen, and hot-blooded lords,
  Whose very dogs would execrations howl
  Against his lineage; not one breast affords
  Him any mercy in that mansion foul,
Save one old beldame, weak in body and in soul.

Ah, happy chance! the aged creature came,
Shuffling along with ivory-headed wand,
To where he stood, hid from the torch's flame,
Behind a broad hall pillar, far beyond
The sound of merriment and chorus bland.
He startled her: but soon she knew his face,
And grasped his fingers in her palsied hand,
Saying, 'Mercy, Porphyro! hie thee from his place,
They are all here to-night, the whole blood-thirsty race!

'Get hence! get hence! there's dwarfish Hildebrand:
He had a fever late, and in the fit
He cursèd thee and thine, both house and land:
Then there's that old Lord Maurice, not a whit
More tame for his grey hairs – Alas me! flit!
Flit like a ghost away.' – 'Ah, Gossip dear,
We're safe enough; here in this arm-chair sit,
And tell me how' – 'Good Saints! not here, not here;
Follow me, child, or else these stones will be thy bier.'

He follow'd through a lowly archèd way,
Brushing the cobwebs with his lofty plume;
And as she muttered 'Well-a – well-a-day!'
He found him in a little moonlight room,
Pale, latticed, chill, and silent as a tomb.
'Now tell me, Angela, by the holy loom
Which none but secret sisterhood may see,
When they St Agnes' wool are weaving piously.'

'St Agnes! Ah! it is St Agnes' Eve –
Yet men will murder upon holy days.
Thou must hold water in a witch's sieve,
And be liege-lord of all the Elves and Fays
To venture so: it fills me with amaze
To see thee, Porphyro! – St Agnes' Eve!
God's help! my lady fair the conjurer plays
This very night: good angels her deceive!
But let me laugh awhile, I've mickle time to grieve.'

Feebly she laugheth in the languid moon,
While Porphyro upon her face doth look,
Like puzzled urchin on an aged crone
Who keepeth closed a wondrous riddle-book,
As spectacled she sits in chimney nook.
But soon his eyes grew brilliant, when she told
His lady's purpose; and he scarce could brook
Tears, at the thought of those enchantments cold,
And Madeline asleep in lap of legends old.

Sudden a thought came like a full-blown rose,
Flushing his brow, and in his painèd heart
Made purple riot: then doth he propose
A stratagem, that makes the beldame start:
'A cruel man and impious thou art!
Sweet lady! let her pray, and sleep, and dream
Alone with her good angels, far apart
From wicked men like thee. Go, go! – I deem
Thou canst not surely be the same that thou didst seem.'

'I will not harm her, by all saints I swear!'
Quoth Porphyro: 'O may I ne'er find grace
When my weak voice shall whisper its last prayer,
If one of her soft ringlets I displace,
Or look with ruffian passion in her face.
Good Angela, believe me, by these tears;
Or I will, even in a moment's space,
Awake, with horrid shout, my foemen's ears,
And beard them, though they be more fang'd than wolves and
bears.'

'Ah! why wilt thou affright a feeble soul?
A poor, weak, palsy-stricken, churchyard thing,
Whose passing-bell may ere the midnight toll;
Whose prayers for thee, each morn and evening,
Were never missed.' Thus plaining, doth she bring
A gentler speech from burning Porphyro;
So woeful, and of such deep sorrowing,
That Angela gives promise she will do
Whatever he shall wish, betide her weal or woe.

Which was, to lead him, in close secrecy,
Even to Madeline's chamber, and there hide
Him in a closet, of such privacy
That he might see her beauty unespied,
And win perhaps that night a peerless bride,
While legioned fairies paced the coverlet,
And pale enchantment held her sleepy-eyed.
Never on such a night have lovers met,
Since Merlin paid his Demon all the monstrous debt.

'It shall be as thou wishest,' said the Dame:
'All cates and dainties shall be storèd there
Quickly on this feast-night: by the tambour frame
Her own lute thou wilt see: no time to spare,
For I am slow and feeble, and scarce dare
On such a catering trust my dizzy head.
Wait here, my child, with patience; kneel in prayer
The while. Ah! thou must needs the lady wed,
Or may I never leave my grave among the dead.'

So saying, she hobbled off with busy fear.
The lover's endless minutes slowly passed;
The dame return'd, and whispered in his ear
To follow her; with aged eyes aghast
From fright of dim espial. Safe at last
Through many a dusky gallery, they gain
The maiden's chamber, silken, hushed, and chaste;
Where Porphyro took covert, pleased amain.
His poor guide hurried back with agues in her brain.

Her faltering hand upon the balustrade,
Old Angela was feeling for the stair,
When Madeline, St Agnes' charmèd maid,
Rose, like a mission'd spirit, unaware:
With silver taper's light, and pious care,
She turned, and down the aged gossip led
To a safe level matting. Now prepare,
Young Porphyro, for gazing on that bed;
She comes, she comes again, like ring-dove frayed and fled.

Out went the taper as she hurried in;
Its little smoke, in pallid moonshine, died:
She closed the door, she panted, all akin
To spirits of the air, and visions wide:
No uttered syllable, or, woe betide!
But to her heart, her heart was voluble,
Paining with eloquence her balmy side;
As though a tongueless nightingale should swell
Her throat in vain, and die, heart-stifled, in her dell.

A casement high and triple-arch'd there was,
All garlanded with carven imageries,
Of fruits and flowers, and bunches of knot-grass,
And diamonded with panes of quaint device,
Innumerable of stains and spendid dyes,
As are the tiger-moth's deep-damasked wings;
And in the midst, 'mong thousand heraldries,
And twilight saints, and dim emblazonings,
A shielded scutcheon blushed with blood of queens and kings.

Full on this casement shone the wintry moon,
And threw warm gules on Madeline's fair breast,
As down she knelt for Heaven's grace and boon;
Rose-bloom fell on her hands, together prest,
And on her silver cross soft amethyst,
And on her hair a glory, like a saint:
She seemed a splendid angel, newly drest,
Save wings, for heaven: – Porphyro grew faint:
She knelt, so pure a thing, so free from mortal taint.

Anon his heart revives: her vespers done,
Of all its wreathèd pearls her hair she frees;
Unclasps her warmèd jewels one by one;
Loosens her fragrant boddice; by degrees
Her rich attire creeps rustling to her knees:
Half-hidden, like a mermaid in sea-weed,
Pensive awhile she dreams awake, and sees,
In fancy, fair St Agnes in her bed,
But dares not look behind, or all the charm is fled.

Soon, trembling in her soft and chilly nest,
In sort of wakeful swoon, perplexed she lay,
Until the poppied warmth of sleep oppressed
Her soothed limbs, and soul fatigued away.
Flown, like a thought, until the morrow-day;
Blissfully havened both from joy and pain;
Clasped like a missal where swart Paynims pray;
Blinded alike from sunshine and from rain,
As though a rose should shut, and be a bud again.

Stolen to this paradise, and so entranced,
Porphyro gazed upon her empty dress,
And listened to her breathing, if it chanced
To wake into a slumberous tenderness;
Which when he heard, that minute did he bless,
And breathed himself: then from the closet crept,
Noiseless as fear in a wide wilderness,
And over the hushed carpet, silent, stept,
And 'tween the curtains peeped, where, lo! – how fast she slept!

Then by the bed-side, where the faded moon
Made a dim, silver twilight, soft he set
A table, and, half anguished, threw thereon
A cloth of woven crimson, gold, and jet: –
O for some drowsy Morphean amulet!
The boisterous, midnight, festive clarion,
The kettle-drum, and far-heard clarionet,
Affray his ears, though but in dying tone: –
The hall-door shuts again, and all the noise is gone.

And still she slept an azure-lidded sleep,
In blanchèd linen, smooth and lavendered,
While he from forth the closet brought a heap
Of candied apple, quince, and plum, and gourd;
With jellies soother than the creamy curd,
And lucent syrops, tinct with cinnamon;
Manna and dates, in argosy transferr'd
From Fez; and spicèd dainties, every one,
From silken Samarcand to cedared Lebanon.

These delicates he heaped with glowing hand
On golden dishes and in baskets bright
Of wreathèd silver: sumptuous they stand
In the retired quiet of the night,
Filling the chilly room with perfume light. –
'And now, my love, my seraph fair, awake!
Thou art my heaven, and I thine eremite:
Open thine eyes, for meek St Agnes' sake,
Or I shall drowse beside thee, so my soul doth ache.'

Thus whispering, his warm, unnervèd arm
Sank in her pillow. Shaded was her dream
By the dusk curtains: – 'twas a midnight charm
Impossible to melt as icèd stream:
The lustrous salvers in the moonlight gleam;
Broad golden fringe upon the carpet lies:
It seemed he never, never could redeem
From such a steadfast spell his lady's eyes;
So mused awhile, entoil'd in woofèd phantasies.

Awakening up, he took her hollow lute, –
Tumultuous, – and, in chords that tenderest be,
He played an ancient ditty, long since mute,
In Provence called 'La belle dame sans mercy':
Close to her ear touching the melody; –
Wherewith disturbed, she uttered a soft moan:
He ceased – she panted quick – and suddenly,
Her blue affrayèd eyes wide open shone:
Upon his knees he sank, pale as smooth-sculptured stone.

Her eyes were open, but she still beheld,
Now wide awake, the vision of her sleep:
There was a painful change, that nigh expelled
The blisses of her dream so pure and deep
At which fair Madeline began to weep,
And moan forth witless words with many a sigh,
While still her gaze on Porphyro would keep;
Who knelt, with joinèd hands and piteous eye,
Fearing to move or speak, she looked so dreamingly.

'Ah, Porphyro!' said she, 'but even now
Thy voice was at sweet tremble in mine ear,
Made tunable with every sweetest vow;
And those sad eyes were spiritual and clear:
How changed thou art! how pallid, chill, and drear!
Give me that voice again, my Porphyro,
Those looks immortal, those complainings dear!
O leave me not in this eternal woe,
For if thou diest, my Love, I know not where to go.'

Beyond a mortal man impassioned far
At these voluptuous accents, he arose,
Ethereal, flushed, and like a throbbing star
Seen 'mid the sapphire heaven's deep repose;
Into her dream he melted, as the rose
Blendeth its odour with the violet, –
Solution sweet: meantime the frost-wind blows
Like Love's alarum pattering the sharp sleet
Against the window-panes; St Agnes' moon hath set.

'Tis dark: quick pattereth the flaw-blown sleet,
'This is no dream, my bride, my Madeline!'
'Tis dark: the icèd gusts still rave and beat:
'No dream, alas! alas! and woe is mine!
Porphyro will leave me here to fade and pine.
Cruel! what traitor could thee hither bring?
I curse not, for my heart is lost in thine,
Though thou forsakest a deceivèd thing; –
A dove forlorn and lost with sick unprunèd wing.'

'My Madeline! sweet dreamer! lovely bride!
Say, may I be for aye thy vassal blest?
Thy beauty's shield, heart-shaped and vermeil-dyed?
Ah, silver shrine, here will I take my rest
After so many hours of toil and quest,
A famished pilgrim, – saved by miracle.
Though I have found, I will not rob thy nest,
Saving of thy sweet self; if thou thinkest well
To trust, fair Madeline, to no rude infidel.

'Hark! 'tis an elfin storm from faery land,
Of haggard seeming, but a boon indeed:
Arise – arise! the morning is at hand; –
The bloated wassailers will never heed: –
Let us away, my love, with happy speed;
There are no ears to hear, or eyes to see, –
Drowned all in Rhenish and the sleepy mead.
Awake! arise! my love, and fearless be,
For o'er the southern moors I have a home for thee.'

She hurried at his words, beset with fears,
For there were sleeping dragons all around,
At glaring watch, perhaps, with ready spears.
Down the wide stairs a darkling way they found;
In all the house was heard no human sound.
A chain-drooped lamp was flickering by each door;
The arras, rich with horsemen, hawk, and hound,
Fluttered in the besieging wind's uproar;
And the long carpets rose along the gusty floor.

They glide, like phantoms, into the wide hall;
Like phantoms to the iron porch they glide,
Where lay the Porter, in uneasy sprawl,
With a huge empty flagon by his side:
The wakeful bloodhound rose, and shook his hide,
But his sagacious eye an inmate owns:
By one, and one, the bolts full easy slide: –
The chains lie silent on the footworn stones;
The key turns, and the door upon its hinges groans.

And they are gone: ay, ages long ago
These lovers fled away into the storm.
That night the Baron dreamt of many a woe,
And all his warrior-guests with shade and form
Of witch, and demon, and large coffin-worm,
Were long be-nightmared. Angela the old
Died palsy-twitched, with meagre face deform;
The Beadsman, after thousand aves told,
For aye unsought-for slept among his ashes cold.

John Keats (1795–1821)

Celia

Were Celia absent and remembrance brought
Her and past raptures thick upon my thought,
The next kind She might meet my raised desire,
And beastly lust quench love's disabled fire.
But when I want my friend, when my vexed heart
Beats short, and pants, and seeks its nobler part,
For the said ill no medicine can be found:
'Tis you that made, 'tis you must cure the wound.

Matthew Prior (1664–1721)

FROM THE CRADLE
TO THE GRAVE

'Ah let me in thy bosom still enjoy
Oblivion of the past'
Theodore Wratislaw

Fat Molly

I was fostered out to a woman called Fat Molly:
It was in the year 744
On the other side of the forest from the monk-fort at Kells
Where the bird-men were scribing their magnificent comic
The Book of Kells.
I'd say Molly was about thirty when I went to her
And she taught me the art of passionate kissing:
From minuscule kisses to majuscule
On lips, breast, neck, shoulders, lips,
And the enwrapping of tongue around tongue.
I was about fourteen
And she used make me kiss her for hours non-stop
And I'd sit in her lap with my hands
Around her waist gulping her down
And eating her green apples
That hung in bunches from her thighs
And the clusters of hot grapes between her breasts
Until from the backs of my ears down to my toes
All of me tingled
And in the backs of her eyes I saw that her glass had no bottom;
Nothing in life afterwards ever tasted quite so luscious
As Fat Molly's kisses;
                        O spirals of animals,
Interlaces of birds;
Sweet, warm, wet, were the kisses she kissed;
Juicy oranges on a naked platter.

She lived all alone in a crannóg
Which had an underwater zig-zag causeway
And people said – and it was not altogether a fiction –
That only a completely drunk man
Could successfully negotiate Fat Molly's entrance;
Completely drunk, I used to stagger home
And fall asleep in the arms of her laughter:
Oh sweet crucifixion, crucified on each other.

Well, that was half a century ago
And now the Vikings are here –
Bloody foreigners –
And there's nothing but blood in the air:
But thank you Fat Molly for a grand education;
Like all great education it was perfectly useless.

Paul Durcan (1944–)

To a Sicilian boy

Love, I adore the contours of thy shape,
Thine exquisite breasts and arms adorable;
The wonders of thine heavenly throat compel
Such fire of love as even my dreams escape:
I love thee as the sea-foam loves the cape,
Or as the shore the sea's enchanting spell:
In sweets the blossoms of thy mouth excel
The tenderest bloom of peach or purple grape.

I love thee, sweet! Kiss me again, again!
Thy kisses soothe me, as tired earth the rain;
Between thine arms I find mine only bliss;
Ah let me in thy bosom still enjoy
Oblivion of the past, divinest boy,
And the dull ennui of a woman's kiss!

Theodore Wratislaw (fl. 1850–90)

Song

Love a woman? You're an ass!
  'Tis a most insipid passion
To choose out for your happiness
  The silliest part of God's creation.

Let the porter and the groom,
  Things designed for dirty slaves,
Drudge in fair Aurelia's womb
  To get supplies for age and graves.

Farewell, woman! I intend
  Henceforth every night to sit
With my lewd, well-natured friend,
  Drinking to engender wit.

Then give me health, wealth, mirth, and wine,
  And, if busy love entrenches,
There's a sweet, soft page of mine
  Does the trick worth forty wenches.

John Wilmot, Earl of Rochester (1647–80)

Late-flowering lust

My head is bald, my breath is bad,
    Unshaven is my chin,
I have not now the joys I had
    When I was young in sin.

I run my fingers down your dress
    With brandy-certain aim
And you respond to my caress
    And maybe feel the same.

But I've a picture of my own
    On this reunion night,
Wherein two skeletons are shewn
    To hold each other tight;

Dark sockets look on emptiness
    Which once was loving-eyed,
The mouth that opens for a kiss
    Has got no tongue inside.

I cling to you inflamed with fear
    As now you cling to me,
I feel how frail you are my dear
    And wonder what will be –

A week? or twenty years remain?
    And then – what kind of death?
A losing fight with frightful pain
    Or a gasping fight for breath?

Too long we let our bodies cling,
    We cannot hide disgust
At all the thoughts that in us spring
    From this late-flowering lust.

John Betjeman (1906–84)

The second rapture

No, worldling, no, 'tis not thy gold
Which thou dost use but to behold,
Nor fortune, honour, nor long life,
Children or friends, nor a good wife
That makes thee happy: these things be
But shadows of felicity.
Give me a wench about thirteen,
Already voted to the queen
Of lust and lovers; whose soft hair
Fanned with the breath of gentle air
O'erspreads her shoulders like a tent
And is her veil and ornament;
Whose tender touch will make the blood
Wild in the aged and the good;
Whose kisses, fastened to the mouth
Of threescore years and longer slouth,
Renew the age; and whose bright eye
Obscures those lesser lights of sky;
Whose snowy breasts (if we may call
That snow that never melts at all)
Makes Jove invent a new disguise
In spite of Juno's jealousies;
Whose every part doth reinvite
The old, decayed, appetite;
And in whose sweet embraces I
May melt myself to lust, and die.
   This is true bliss, and I confess
   There is no other happiness.

Thomas Carew (1595?–1639)

204

Friendship

When we were charming *Backfisch*
    With curls and velvet bows
We shared a charming kitten
    With tiny velvet toes.

It was so gay and playful;
    It flew like a woolly ball
From my lap to your shoulder –
    And, oh, it was so small,

So warm – and so obedient
    If we cried; 'That's enough!'
It lay and slept between us,
    A purring ball of fluff.

But now that I am thirty
    And she is thirty-one,
I shudder to discover
    How wild our cat has run.

It's bigger than a Tiger,
    It's eyes are jets of flame,
Its claws are gleaming daggers,
    Could it have once been tame?

Take it away; I'm frightened!
    But she, with placid brow,
Cries: 'This is our Kitty-witty!
    Why don't you love her now?'

Katherine Mansfield (1888–1923)

A song of a young lady to her ancient lover

Ancient person, for whom I
All the flattering youth defy,
Long it be ere thou grow old,
Aching, shaking, crazy cold,
But still continue as thou art,
Ancient person of my heart.

On thy withered lips and dry,
Which like barren furrows lie,
Brooding kisses I will pour
Shall thy youthful heat restore.
Such kind showers in Autumn fall,
And a second Spring recall,
Nor from thee will ever part,
Ancient person of my heart.

Thy nobler part, which but to name,
In our sex would be counted shame,
By age's frozen grasp possessed,
From his ice shall be released,
And, soothed by my reviving hand,
In former warmth and vigour stand.
All a lover's wish can reach,
For thy joy my love shall teach,
And for thy pleasure shall improve
All that art can add to love.
Yet still I love thee without art,
Ancient person of my heart.

John Wilmot, Earl of Rochester (1647–80)

Epigrams XXIX

Phyllis, when your old claws attempt to strum
My instrument, I'm half-throttled by your thumb,
And when you call me 'mouse' or 'precious
lover'
It takes me over twelve hours to recover.
You've no idea how to make love. Say, 'Please
Accept a hundred thousand sesterces'
Or, 'Have some farmland – here's a large estate
In Setia' or, 'Take this antique plate,
My wines, slaves, tables, or my house in town.'
That's the right way to rub me – up, not down.

Martial (c. AD 40–c. 104)
(Trans. James Michie)

from Hero and Leander

With that he stripped him to the ivory skin,
And crying, 'Love, I come,' leapt lively in.
Whereat the sapphire-visaged god grew proud,
And made his capering Triton sound aloud,
Imagining that Ganymede, displeased,
Had left the heavens; therefore on him he seized.
Leander strived, the waves about him wound,
And pulled him to the bottom, where the ground
Was strewed with pearl, and in low coral groves
Sweet singing mermaids sported with their loves
On heaps of heavy gold, and took great pleasure
To spurn in careless sort the shipwrack treasure.
For here the stately azure palace stood,
Where kingly Neptune and his train abode.
The lusty god embraced him, called him 'love,'
And swore he never should return to Jove.
But when he knew it was not Ganymede,
For under water he was almost dead,
He heaved him up, and looking on his face
Beat down the bold waves with his triple mace,
Which mounted up, intending to have kissed him,
And fell in drops like tears because they missed him.
Leander being up, began to swim,
And looking back, saw Neptune follow him;
Whereat aghast, the poor soul 'gan to cry,
'O let me visit Hero ere I die.'
The god put Helle's bracelet on his arm,
And swore the sea should never do him harm.
He clapped his plump cheeks, with his tresses played,
And smiling wantonly, his love bewrayed.
He watched his arms, and as they opened wide,
At every stroke, betwixt them would he slide,
And steal a kiss, and then run out and dance,
And as he turned, cast many a lustful glance,
And throw him gaudy toys to please his eye,
And dive into the water, and there pry

Upon his breast, his thighs, and every limb,
And up again, and close beside him swim,
And talk of love. Leander made reply,
'You are deceived, I am no woman, I.'

Christopher Marlowe (1564–93)

from Goblin market

She cried 'Laura,' up the garden,
'Did you miss me?
Come and kiss me.
Never mind my bruises,
Hug me, kiss me, suck my juices
Squeezed from goblin fruits for you,
Goblin pulp and goblin dew.
Eat me, drink me, love me;
Laura, make much of me:
For your sake I have braved the glen
And had to do with goblin merchant men.'

Laura started from her chair,
Flung her arms up in the air,
clutched her hair:
'Lizzie, Lizzie, have you tasted
For my sake the fruit forbidden?
Must your light like mine be hidden,
Your young life like mine be wasted,
Undone in mine undoing
And ruined in my ruin,
Thirsty, cankered, goblin-ridden?' –
She clung about her sister,
Kissed and kissed and kissed her:
Tears once again
Refreshed her shrunken eyes,
Dropping like rain
After long sultry drouth;
Shaking with anguish fear, and pain,
She kissed and kissed her with a hungry mouth.

Christina Rossetti (1830–94)

The days of my youth

My days of youth are over – my torch of life is out.
What used to be my sex-appeal is now my water-spout.
Time was when by its own accord 'twould from my trousers
spring –
But now I have a wholetime job to find the blasted thing.

It used to be embarrassing the way it would behave
For early in the morning it would stand and watch me shave –
But as old age approaches, it sure gives me the blues
To see it hang its withered head and watch me clean my shoes.

Anon

Epigram

(after *The Harp that Once Through Tara's Halls*)

The prick that once through Fanny's drawers,
    The soul of fucking shed,
Now hangs as mute as these two balls,
    As if that soul were dead.

My penis now so seldom stands,
    The only throb it gives,
Is when I rub it in my hands,
    To prove that still it lives.

Anon

Gather ye rosebuds

Gather ye rosebuds while ye may.
Old time is still a-flying.
And the pecker which is stiff today
Tomorrow will be dying.

Anon

An old prostitute from Marseilles

An old prostitute from Marseilles,
Douched with a rotary spray.
  Said she, 'Ah, that's better
  I've found that French letter
That's been missing since Armistice Day.'

Anon

COMIC RELIEF

'But all my verses really owe
Their wit and charm and all their salt
To spicy, merry, sexy flow'
Catullus

A candle

There is a thing which in the light
Is seldom used; but in the night
It serves the maiden female crew,
The ladies, and the goodwives too.
They use to take it in their hand,
And then it will uprightly stand;
And to a hole they it apply,
Where by its goodwill it would die:
It spends, goes out, and still within
It leaves its moisture thick and thin.

Sir John Suckling (1609–42)

Upon the author of the play called *Sodom*

Tell me, abandoned miscreant, prithee tell,
What damned power, invoked and sent from Hell
(If Hell were bad enough) did thee inspire
To write what fiends ashamed would blushing hear?
Hast thou of late embraced some succubus,
And used the lewd familiar for a Muse?
Or didsty thy soul by inch o' the candle sell,
To gain the glorious name of pimp to Hell?
If so go, and its vowed allegiance swear,
Without press-money, be its volunteer:
May he who envies thee deserve thy fate,
Deserve both heaven's and mankind's scorn and hate.
Disgrace to libels! Foil to very shame!
Whom 'tis a scandal to vouchsafe to damn!
What foul description's foul enough for thee,
Sunk quite below the reach of infamy?
Thou covetest to be lewd, but want'st the might
And art all over devil, but in wit.
Weak feeble strainer at mere ribaldry,
Whose Muse is impotent to that degree,
It had need, like age, to be whipped to lechery.

Vile sot! who clapped with poetry art sick,
And void'st corruption like a shankered prick,
Like ulcers, thy impostumed addle brains
Drop out in matter, which thy paper stains:
Whence nauseous rhymes by filthy births proceed,
As maggots in some turd-engendering breed.
Thy Muse has got the flowers, and they ascend
As in some greensick girl, at upper end.
Sure Nature made, or meant at least to have done't,
Thy tongue a clitoris, thy mouth a cunt.
How well a dildo would that place become,
To gag it up, and make it forever dumb!

At least it should be syringed –
Or wear some stinking merkin for a beard,
That all from its base converse might be scared:
As they a door shut up, and mark 't beware,
That tells infection, and the Plague is there.

Thou Moorfields author! fit for bawds to quote
(If bawds themselves with honour safe may do't)
When suburb-prentice comes to hire delight,
And wants incentives to dull appetite,
There punk, perhaps, may thy brave works rehearse,
Frigging the senseless thing with hand and verse;
Which after shall (preferred to dressing-box)
Hold turpentine and medicines for the pox:
Or (if I may ordain a fate more fit
For such foul, nasty excrements of wit)
May they, condemned, to the public jakes be lent,
(For me, I'd fear the piles of vengeance sent
Should I with them profane my fundament)
There bugger wiping porters when they shite,
And so thy book itself turn sodomite.

John Oldham (1653–83)

Epitaph for Oscar Wilde

Earth to earth, sod to sod,
That's how Oscar greets his God.
It was for sinners such as this
That God made Hell bottomless.

Attributed to Charles Algernon
Swinburne (1837–1909)

Lady H— to Mrs P—

Said old Lady H—, once a blooming young wench,
　　But whose head's now adorned with gray hairs,
'I admire the great comfort and taste which the French
　　Combine in their fashions of chairs;
For English, our frames are both simple and neat;
　　Yet the French in past times were so puffed,
That our bottoms were never considered complete,
　　Until sent o'er to France to be stuffed.'

Anon

The harlot of Jerusalem

(Song)

Down in the land of King Farouk
there lived a girl of ill-repute,
a prostitute, a bloody beaut,
the harlot of Jerusalem.

Kafoozalum was a wily witch,
a warty whore, a brazen bitch,
who caused all the pricks to itch,
right throughout Jerusalem.

The floors, the halls, the Wailing Wall,
were all festooned with the balls
and tools of fools who tried to ride
the harlot of Jerusalem.

And though she'd whored for many a year,
of pregnancy she had no fear;
she washed her passage out with beer,
the best in all Jerusalem.

A student lived beneath the wall,
and though he'd only got one ball,
he'd been through all, or nearly all
the harlots of Jerusalem.

His phallic limb was lean and tall,
his sex technique caused all to fall;
his victims lined the Wailing Wall
that runs around Jerusalem.

One night returning from a spree,
although he didn't have the fee,
he decided then and there to see
the harlot of Jerusalem.

He walked in through the brothel door
and laid her on the earthen floor,
to have his fill of that old whore
the harlot of Jerusalem.

He took her to a shady nook
and from his pants he gently took
a penis like a butcher's hook,
the pride of all Jerusalem.

He whopped it up between her thighs,
it damn near reached up to her eyes,
but all she gave was a couple of sighs,
the harlot of Jerusalem.

It was a sight to make you sick
to hear him grunt so fast and quick
while rending with his crooked prick
the womb of fair Kafoozalum.

But then there came an Israelite,
a lusty, boasting, bragging skite,
who'd vowed that he would spend that night
with the harlot of Jerusalem.

It was for her no fortune good
that he should want to flash his pud;
he mostly hung about the wood
and perved on all Jerusalem.

He loathed the art of copulation,
for his delight was masturbation,
for which he'd pay with great elation
the whores of old Jerusalem.

And though he paid his women well,
this syphilitic spawn of hell,
somehow each year they tolled the bell
for ten whores of Jerusalem.

So when he saw the grunting pair,
with roars of rage he rent the air,
and vowed that he would soon take care
of the harlot of Jerusalem.

Upon the earth he found a stick
to which he fastened half a brick
and took a swipe at the mighty prick
of the student of Jerusalem.

He gave the pair a dirty look
and grabbed the student by his crook
and tossed him into Kedron's brook
that flows hard by Jerusalem.

The student gave a mighty roar
and swore he'd even up the score;
in the harlot's arse a hole he bore
that even stretched Kafoozalum.

He stepped back full of rage and fight
and grabbed the perving Israelite,
and rammed him up with all his might
the arsehole of Kafoozalum.

The wily whore she knew her part;
she gave a squeeze and blew a fart
that sent him flying like a dart
right across Jerusalem.

Across the sea of Galilee
he was buzzing like a bumblebee,
till he caught his balls upon a tree
that grows in old Jerusalem.

And to this day you still can see
his balls a-hanging in that tree;
let that to you a warning be
when passing through Jerusalem.

As for the student and his lass,
many a playful night did pass
until she joined the VD class
for harlots in Jerusalem.

And even then the randy slut
would leave the town and work her butt
beside the Salvation Army hut
in the old part of Jerusalem.

This harlot lived for many a year
till sterilised by gonorrhoea,
and men of taste would not go near
the harlot of Jerusalem.

But all you other randy folk
who love to have your nightly poke
can still pay the fee and let it soak
in the harlot of Jerusalem.

Anon

O'Reilly's daughter

(Song)

Sitting in O'Reilly's bar
I was a-drinking gin and water;
suddenly it came to mind:
I'd like to shag O'Reilly's daughter.

Her hair was black, her eyes were blue,
the colonel, major and captain sought her,
the company goat and the drummer too,
but they never got into O'Reilly's daughter.

O Jack O'Sullivan is my name,
I'm the king of copulation,
drinking gin my claim to fame,
shagging girls my occupation.

Well, walking through the park that day
who should I meet but O'Reilly's daughter;
never a word I had to say
but, 'Don't you think we really oughter?'

Up the stairs and into bed,
I gently cocked my left leg over;
never a word the maiden said,
laughed like hell till the fun was over.

I banged her till her tits were flat,
filled her up with soapy water
enough to make a dozen brats –
if she doesn't have twins she really oughter.

Heard some footsteps on the stair,
who should it be but her bloody old father?
Two horse-pistols in his belt,
looking for the man who'd had his daughter.

Grabbed O'Reilly by the hair,
shoved his face in a bucket of water,
rammed the pistols up his butt
a damn sight harder than I shagged his daughter.

Now O'Reilly's dead and gone,
now O'Reilly is no more;
we've got hold of his coffin lid,
going to use it for a door.

Now come ye lasses, come ye maids,
answer now and don't speak shyly:
would yez have it straight and true,
or the way I give it to the one-eyed Reilly?

Anon

Eskimo Nell

When a man grows old and his balls grow cold,
And the end of his knob turns blue,
When it's bent in the middle like a one-string fiddle,
He can tell you a yarn or two:
So find me a seat and stand me a beer,
And a tale to you I'll tell,
Of Deadeye Dick and Mexico Pete,
And the harlot named Eskimo Nell.
Now when Deadeye Dick and Mexico Pete
Go forth in search of fun,
It's usually Dick who wields the prick,
And Mexico Pete the gun;
And when Deadeye Dick and Mexico Pete
Are sore, depressed and sad,
It's usually a cunt that bears the brunt,
Though the shootin' ain't too bad.
Well, Deadeye Dick and Mexico Pete
Had been hunting in Dead Man's Creek,
And they'd had no luck in the way of a fuck
For nigh on half a week;
Just a moose or two, or a caribou,
Or a reindeer or a doe,
And for Deadeye Dick with his kingly prick,
Fuckin' was mighty slow.
So do or die, he adjusted his fly,
And set out for the Rio Grande,
Deadeye Dick with his muscular prick,
And Pete with his gun in his hand.
And so they blazed a randy trail,
No man their path withstood,
And many a bride who was hubby's pride
Knew pregnant widowhood.
They made the strand of the Rio Grande
At the height of a blazing noon,
And to slake their thirst and to do their worst,
They went into Black Mike's saloon.

And as the door swung open wide,
Both prick and gun flashed free;
'According to sex, you bleeding wrecks,
You drinks or fucks with me.'
Now they'd heard of the prick called Deadeye Dick,
From the Horn to Panama,
And with nothing worse than a muttered curse
Those dagoes sought the bar;
The women too knew his playful ways,
Down on the Rio Grande,
And forty whores took down their drawers
At Deadeye Dick's command.
They saw the finger of Mexico Pete
Twitch on the trigger grip;
They dared not wait; at a fearful rate,
Those whores began to strip.
Now Deadeye Dick was breathing quick,
With lecherous snorts and grunts.
As forty arses were bared to view,
To say nothing of forty cunts.
Now forty arses and forty cunts,
You'll agree if you use your wits,
With a little bit of arithmetic,
Make exactly eighty tits;
And eighty tits make a gladsome sight
For a man with a raging stand,
It may be rare in Berkeley Square,
But not on the Rio Grande.
Our Deadeye Dick, he fucks 'em quick,
So he backed up and took his run,
And made a dart at the nearest tart,
And scores a hole in one.
He threw the whore to the sawdust floor,
And fucked her deep and fine,
And though she grinned it put the wind
Up the other thirty-nine.
Our Deadeye Dick, he fucks 'em quick,
And flinging the first aside,
He was making a pass at the second arse
When the swing doors opened wide,

And entered in, to that hall of sin
Into that harlot-hell,
All unafraid, strode a gentle maid
Whose name was Eskimo Nell.
Our Deadeye Dick, who fucks 'em quick,
Was well into number two,
When Eskimo Nell lets out a yell
And says to him, 'Hey, you!'
That hefty lout, he turned about,
Both nob and face were red,
And with a single flick of his muscular prick
The whore flew over his head.
But Eskimo Nell she took it well,
And looked him straight in the eyes,
With the utmost scorn she sneered at his horn
As it rose from his hairy thighs.
She blew a drag from her smouldering fag
Over his steaming nob,
And so utterly beat was Mexico Pete
He forgot to do his job.
It was Eskimo Nell who broke the spell
In accents calm and cool,
'You cunt-struck shrimp of a Yankee pimp,
D'you call that thing a tool?
If this here town can't wear that down,'
She sneered to the squirming whores,
'There's one little cunt that will do the stunt,
That's Eskimo Nell's, not yours.'
She shed her garments one by one
With an air of conscious pride;
Till at last she stood in her womanhood,
And they saw the Great Divide.
She lay down there on the table bare,
Where someone had left a glass,
And with a twitch of her tits, she crushed it to bits
Between the cheeks of her arse.
She bent her knees with supple ease,
And opened her legs apart,
And with a final nod at the waiting sod,
She gave him his cue to start.

But Deadeye Dick with his kingly prick
Prepared to take his time,
For a girl like this was fucking bliss,
So he staged a pantomime.
He winked his arsehole in and out,
And made his balls inflate,
Until they rose like granite globes
On top of a garden gate.
He rubbed his foreskin up and down,
His knob increased its size;
His mighty prick grew twice as thick,
Till it almost reached his eyes;
He polished the nob with rum and gob
To make it steaming hot,
And to finish the job he sprinkled the nob
With a cayenne pepper pot.
He didn't back up to take a run,
Nor yet a flying leap,
But bent right down and came alongside
With a steady forward creep.
Then he took a sight as a gunman might
Along his mighty tool,
And shoved in his lust with a dexterous thrust,
Firm, calculating and cool.
Have you ever seen the pistons
On the giant CPR?
With the driving force of a thousand horse?
Then you know what pistons are;
Or you think you do, but you've yet to view
The awe-inspiring trick,
Of the work that's done on a non-stop run
By a man like Deadeye Dick.
But Eskimo Nell was an infidel,
She equalled a whole harem,
With the strength of ten in her abdomen,
And her rock-of-ages beam;
Amidships she could stand the rush
Like the flush of a water closet,
And she grasped his cock like a Chatswood lock
On the National Safe Deposit.

She lay for a while with a subtle smile,
While the grip of her cunt grew keener,
Then she gave a sigh and sucked him dry,
With the ease of a vacuum cleaner.
She performed this feat in a way so neat
As to set at complete defiance
The primary cause and the basic laws
That govern sexual science:
She calmly rode through the phallic code,
Which for years had stood the test,
And the ancient rules of the Classic Schools
In a moment or two went west.
And now, my friend, we draw to the end
Of this copulatory epic –
The effect on Dick was sudden and quick,
Akin to an anaesthetic;
He slipped to the floor and he knew no more,
His passion extinct and dead,
Nor did he shout as his tool came out,
It was stripped right down to a thread.
Mexico Pete he sprang to his feet
To avenge his pal's affront,
With a fearful jolt, for he drew his Colt,
And rammed it up into her cunt;
He shoved it up to the trigger grip
And fired three times three,
But to his surprise she rolled her eyes
And squeaked in ecstasy.
She leaped to her feet with a smile so sweet,
'Bully,' she said, 'for you!
Though I might have guessed it's about the best
You flogged-out sods could do.
When next your friend and you intend
To sally forth for fun,
Buy Deadeye Dick a sugar-stick
And get yourself a bun.
And now I'm off to the frozen North
To the land where spunk is spunk,
Not a trickly stream of lukewarm cream,
But a solid frozen chunk.

Back to the land where they understand
What it means to copulate,
Where even the dead lie two in a bed,
And the infants masturbate.
Back to the land of the mighty stand,
Where the nights are six months long,
Where the polar bear wanks off in his lair,
That's where they'll sing this song.
They'll tell this tale on the Arctic trail,
Where the nights are sixty below,
Where it's so damn cold french letters are sold
Wrapped in a ball of snow;
In the Valley of Death with bated breath,
It's there they'll sing it too,
Where the skeletons rattle in sexual battle,
And the mouldy corpses screw!
Back once more to the sins of men,
To the Land of the Midnight Sun,
I go to spend a worthy end
For the north is calling '*Come!*'

Anon

Nine times a night

A stalwart young fellow from London came down
To set up his trade in Ramsbottom town;
They asked who he was and he answered them right,
'I belong to a family called "Nine times a night".'

A buxom young widow who still wore her weeds,
Whose husband had left her her riches and deeds,
Resolvèd she was by her conjugal right,
To fill up her chisum with nine times a night.

She ordered her waiting maids, Betty and Nan,
To keep a lookout for that wonderful man,
And whenever they saw him appear in their sight,
To bring her glad tidings of nine times a night.

Fortune favoured the joke on the very next day,
Those giggling girls saw him coming that way.
Then upstairs they ran with amorous delight,
'Upon my word, madam, here's nine times a night.'

From a chair she arose (what I say is true),
And down to the hall door like lightning they flew,
She viewed him all over and gave him a smack,
The bargain was struck and done in a crack.

The marriage being over, the bride tolled the bell,
He did her six times and pleased her so well,
She vowed from her heart she was satisfied quite,
Still she gave him a hint of nine times a night.

He said, 'My dear bride, you mistook the wrong thing,
I said to that family I did belong.
Nine times a night is too much for a man,
I can't do it myself, but my sister, she can.'

Anon

In Mobile

(Song: to the tune – 'She'll Be Coming Round The Mountain')

O the parson is perverted in Mobile,
O the parson is perverted in Mobile,
O the parson is perverted
and his morals are inverted
and there's thousands he's converted in Mobile.

O the bishop is a bugger in Mobile,
O the bishop is a bugger in Mobile,
O the bishop is a bugger
and his brother is another
and they bugger one another in Mobile.

There's a girl called Lady Dinah in Mobile,
there's a girl called Lady Dinah in Mobile,
there's a girl called Lady Dinah,
and you'll say once you grind her
that she's got the best vagina in Mobile.

There's a shortage of good whores in Mobile,
there's a shortage of good whores in Mobile,
there's a shortage of good whores,
but there's keyholes in the doors,
and knotholes in the floors in Mobile.

Frenchies are in short supply in Mobile,
frenchies are in short supply in Mobile,
frenchies are in short supply
and so that's the reason why
they hang them out to dry in Mobile.

There's no paper in the bogs in Mobile,
there's no paper in the bogs in Mobile,
there's no paper in the bogs,
they just wait until it clogs,
then they saw it off in logs in Mobile.

O they don't use boggus paper in Mobile,
O they don't use boggus paper in Mobile,
they don't use boggus paper,
they don't hold with no such caper,
they just use a putty scraper in Mobile.

Virgins are very rare in Mobile,
virgins are very rare in Mobile,
virgins are very rare
'cos when they get their pubic hair
they get rooted by the mayor in Mobile.

There's a virgin, so they say, in Mobile,
there's a virgin, so they say, in Mobile,
there's a virgin, so they say,
she was born just yesterday,
but the navy's on its way to Mobile.

O the students get no tail in Mobile,
O the students get no tail in Mobile,
O the students get no tail
so they bang it on the rail –
it's the arsehole of creation, is Mobile.

There's a man called Dirty Keith in Mobile,
there's a man called Dirty Keith in Mobile,
there's a man called Dirty Keith
and he wears a laurel wreath
of pubic hairs around his teeth in Mobile.

There's a naughty boy called Danny in Mobile,
there's a naughty boy called Danny in Mobile,
there's a naughty boy called Danny
and he likes his bit of fanny
and he gets it off his granny in Mobile.

There's a stupid man called Green in Mobile,
there's a stupid man called Green in Mobile,
there's a stupid man called Green,
and he thinks he is a queen,
but he's got a ruptured spleen in Mobile.

O the girls all wear tin pants in Mobile,
O the girls all wear tin pants in Mobile,
O the girls all wear tin pants
but they take them off to dance –
everybody gets his chance in Mobile.

There's a lack of fornication in Mobile,
there's a lack of fornication in Mobile,
there's a lack of fornication
but there's lots of masturbation –
and that's the situation in Mobile.

O they have a pet aversion in Mobile,
O they have a pet aversion in Mobile,
the aversion was a virgin
but she didn't take much urgin';
soon the penises were surgin' in Mobile.

O the men they wash the dishes in Mobile,
O the men they wash the dishes in Mobile,
O the men they wash the dishes
and they dry them on their breeches –
O the dirty sons-of-bitches, in Mobile!

O the cows they all are dead in Mobile,
O the cows they all are dead in Mobile,
O the cows they all are dead
so they milk the bulls instead,
because babies must be fed in Mobile.

If you ever go to jail in Mobile,
if you ever go to jail in Mobile,
if you ever go to jail
and you need a piece of tail,
the sheriff's wife's for sale in Mobile.

Gentlemen of the working classes in Mobile,
gentlemen of the working classes in Mobile,
gentlemen of the working classes
when you've finished with your glasses
you can stuff 'em up your arses in Mobile.

When the tax collector calls in Mobile,
when the tax collector calls in Mobile,
when the tax collector calls
they cut off both his balls
and they nail them to the walls in Mobile.

O we won't go back to Subic from Mobile,
O we won't go back to Subic from Mobile,
O we won't go back to Subic –
the mosquitoes there are too big
and they bite you in the pubic in Mobile.

O the girls don't smell like roses in Mobile,
O the girls don't smell like roses in Mobile,
O the girls don't smell like roses
but they know a hundred poses
so you needn't hold your noses in Mobile.

Anon

Gay Furius, Aurelius

I'll fuck you both right up the ass,
Gay Furius, Aurelius,
For saying I'm not chaste, what brass!
Because my poems aren't. Thus
You miss the point; my poetry
Is simply not the same as me.
But all my verses really owe
Their wit and charm and all their salt
To spicy, merry, sexy flow
Of words that even stir up halt
And hairy granddads – no young crew –
Whose stiffened loins can hardly screw.
Well, read my poems: If your brass
Insists my verse makes me like you,
I'll fuck you both right up the ass.

Catullus (c. 84–c.54 BC)
(Trans. R. Meyers & R. J. Ormsby)

from The Prologue to The Wife of Bath's Tale.

(The Canterbury Tales)

Blessed above all other men is he,
That astrologer, Mister Ptolemy.
Who set down in his book, the *Almagest*
This proverb: 'Of all men he is the wisest
Who doesn't care who has the world in hand.'
From which proverb you are to understand
That if you have enough, why should you care
A curse how well-off other people are?
Don't worry, you old dotard – it's all right,
You'll have cunt enough and plenty, every night.
What bigger miser than he who'll not let
Another light a candle at his lantern –
He won't have any the less light, I'm thinking!
If you've enough, what's there to grumble at?
   And you say if we make ourselves look smart
With dresses and expensive jewellery,
It only puts at risk our chastity;
And then, confound you, you must quote this text,
And back yourself up with the words of Paul,
As thus: 'In chaste and modest apparel
You women must adorn yourselves,' said he,
'And not with braided hair and jewellery,
Such as pearls and gold; and not in costly dress.'
But of your text, and your red-letter rubric,
I'll be taking no more notice than a gnat!
   And you said this: that I was like a cat,
For you have only got to singe its skin,
And then the cat will never go from home;
But if its coat is looking sleek and gay,
She won't stop in the house, not half a day,
But off she goes the first thing in the morning,
To show her coat off and go caterwauling.
That's to say, if I'm all dressed up, Mister Brute,
I'll run out in my rags to show them off!

Mister Old Fool, what good is it to spy?
If you begged Argus with his hundred eyes
To be my bodyguard – what better choice? –
There's little he would see unless I let him,
For if it killed me, yet I'd somehow fool him!

And you have also said, there are three things,
Three things there are that trouble the whole earth,
And there's no man alive can stand the fourth –
Sweet Mister Brute, Jesus cut short your life!
You keep on preaching that an odious wife
Is to be counted one of these misfortunes.
Really, are there no other comparisons
That you can make, and without dragging in
A poor innocent wife as one of them?

Then you compare a woman's love to Hell,
To barren lands where rain will never fall.
And you go on to say, it's like Greek fire,
The more it burns, the fiercer its desire
To burn up everything that can be burned.
And just as grubs and worms eat up a tree,
Just so a woman will destroy her husband;
All who are chained to wives know this, you say.

Ladies and gentlemen, just as you've heard
I'd browbeat them; they really thought they'd said
All these things to me in their drunkenness.
All lies – but I'd get Jankin to stand witness
And bear me out, and my young niece also.
O Lord! the pain I gave them, and the woe,
And they, heaven knows, quite innocent of course.
For I could bite and whinny like a horse.
I'd scold them even when I was at fault,
For otherwise I'd often have been dished.
Who comes first to the mill, is first to grind;
I'd get in first, till they'd be glad to find
A quick excuse for things they'd never done
In their whole lives; and so our war was won.
I'd pick on them for wenching; never mind
They were so ill that they could barely stand!

And yet it tickled him to the heart, because
He thought it showed how fond of him I was.

I swore that all my walking out at night
Was to spy out the women that he tapped;
Under that cover, how much fun I had!
To us at birth such mother-wit is given;
As long as they live God has granted women
Three things by nature: lies, and tears, and spinning.
There's one thing I can boast of: in the end
I'd gain, in every way, the upper hand
By force or fraud, or by some stratagem
Like everlasting natter, endless grumbling.
Bed in particular was their misfortune;
That's when I'd scold, and see they got no fun.
I wouldn't stop a moment in the bed
If I felt my husband's arm over my side,
No, not until his ransom had been paid,
And then I'd let him do the thing he liked.
What I say is, everything has its price;
You cannot lure a hawk with empty hand.
If I wanted something, I'd endure his lust.
And even feign an appetite for it;
Though I can't say I ever liked old meat –
And that's what made me nag them all the time.
Even though the Pope were sitting next to them
I'd not spare them at table or at board,
But paid them back, I tell you, word for word.
I swear upon my oath, so help me God,
I owe them not a word, all's been paid back.
I set my wits to work till they gave up;
They had to, for they knew it would be best,
Or else we never would have been at rest.
For even if he looked fierce as a lion,
Yet he would fail to get his satisfaction.
    Then I would turn and say, 'Come, dearest, come!
How meek you look, like Wilkin, dear old lamb!
Come to me, sweetheart, let me kiss your cheek!
You ought to be all patient and meek,
And have ever such a scrupulous consience –
Or so you preach of Job and his patience!
Always be patient; practise what you preach,
For if you don't, we've got a thing to teach,

Which is: it's good to have one's wife in peace!
One of us has got to knuckle under,
And since man is more rational a creature
Than woman is, it's you who must forbear.
But what's the matter now? Why moan and groan?
You want my quim just for yourself alone?
Why, it's all yours – there now, go take it all!
By Peter, but I swear you love it well!
For if I wished to sell my pretty puss,
I'd go about as sweet as any rose;
But no, I'll keep it just for you to taste.
Lord knows you're in the wrong; and that's the truth!'
    All arguments we had were of that kind.
Now I will speak about my fourth husband.
    My fourth husband was a libertine;
That is to say, he kept a concubine;
And I was young, and passionate, and gay,
Stubborn and strong, and merry as a magpie.
How I would dance to the harp's tunable
Music, and sing like any nightingale,
When I had downed a draught of mellow wine!
Metellius, the dirty dog, that swine
Who with a club beat his own wife to death
Because she drank – if I had been his wife,
Even he would not have daunted me from drink!
And after taking wine I'm bound to think
On Venus – sure as cold induces hail,
A greedy mouth points to a greedy tail.
A woman full of wine has no defence,
All lechers know this from experience.
    But, Lord Christ! when it all comes back to me,
And I recall my youth and gaiety,
It warms the very cockles of my heart.
And to this day it does my spirit good
To think that in my time I've had my fling.
But age, alas, that cankers everything,
Has stripped me of my beauty and spirit.
Let it go then! Goodbye, and devil take it!
The flour's all gone; there is no more to say.
Now I must sell the bran as best I may;

But all the same I mean to have my fun.
And now I'll tell about my fourth husband.

   I tell you that it rankled in my heart
That in another he should take delight.
But he was paid for it in full, by God!
From that same wood I made for him a rod –
Not with my body, and not like a slut,
But certainly I carried on with folk
Until I made him stew in his own juice,
With fury, and with purest jealousy.
By God! on earth I was his purgatory,
For which I hope his soul's in Paradise.
God knows he often had to sit and whine
When his shoe pinched him cruellest! And then
How bitterly, and in how many ways,
I wrung his withers, there is none can guess
Or know, save only he and God in heaven!
He died when I came from Jerusalem,
And now lies buried under the rood beam,
Although his tomb is not as gorgeous
As the sepulchre of Darius
That Apelles sculpted so skilfully;
For to have buried him expensively
Would have been waste. So goodbye, and God rest him!
He's in his grave now, shut up in his coffin.

Geoffrey Chaucer (c.1393–1400)
(Trans. D. Wright)

The good ship *Venus*

(Song – to the tune 'In and Out the Window')

It was on the good ship *Venus*,
by Christ you should have seen us;
the figurehead was a whore in bed
astride a rampant penis.

> *Frigging in the rigging,*
> *frigging in the rigging,*
> *we're frigging in the rigging*
> *'cos there's nothing else to do.*

It was at the China station
by way of celebration
we sunk a junk with jets of spunk
by mutual masturbation.

We sailed to the Canaries
to screw the local fairies;
we got the syph in Tenerife
and the clap in Buenos Aires.

We sailed to the Bahamas
where the girls all wear pyjamas;
they wouldn't screw our motley crew –
they much preferred bananas.

The captain's name was Mugger,
a dirty-minded bugger;
he wasn't fit to shovel shit
from one deck to the other.

The first mate's name was Morgan,
a homosexual Gorgon;
six men could ride with legs astride
upon his sexual organ.

The second mate's name was Abel;
his arsehole bore this label:
'I'll give the crew their daily due
though I'm no Betty Grable.'

The third mate's name was Walter;
at love he'd never falter.
The bloody stiff had given syph
to all the girls in Malta.

The stoker was McGuire,
he really was a trier,
for though on shore he kept a whore,
on board he pulled his wire.

The steward's name was Topper;
boy did he have a whopper!
Twice round the deck, once round his neck,
and up his arse for a stopper.

The bosun's name was Andy,
a bastard bald and bandy;
they filled his bum with boiling rum
for pissing in the brandy.

But the bosun's plan was prosperous;
he dipped his cock in phosphorus;
all through the night it kept alight
to guide us throgh the Bosporus.

The purser's name was Lester;
he was a hymen tester;
through hymens thick he'd shove his prick
and leave it there to fester.

That purser came from Wigan;
by God he had a big 'un!
We bashed his cock with a lump of rock
for frigging in the rigging.

The fireman was McTavish,
and young girls he did ravish;
his missing tool's in Istanbul —
he was a trifle lavish.

The carpenter Carruthers,
beloved of all the others;
he wasn't quite hermaphrodite,
but a mistake of his mother's.

The engineer McPherson
to snatch had an aversion;
so he stuck his cock up a water-chock —
a peculiar perversion!

The musician's name was Carter;
he tuned his arse as a farter.
He could play anything from God Save the King
to Beethoven's Moonlight Sonata.

The cook's name was O'Malley,
he didn't dilly-dally;
he shot his bolt with such a jolt
he whitewashed half the galley.

The cook's offsider Riemann,
he was a filthy demon;
he served the crew a filthy brew
of foreskins boiled in semen.

A third cook's name was Aiken;
each morning he'd awaken
and scrape the spunk from off his bunk
to fry the skipper's bacon.

The trainee cook was Wooden,
by Christ he was a good 'un;
he tossed off twice in a bag of rice
and called it sago puddin'.

The radio operator
he was a masturbator;
to get a jolt he'd shoot his bolt
across the oscillator.

A stowaway named Tupper,
we rubbed his balls with butter;
the charge whizzed past the mizzen mast
and foamed against the scupper.

The stewardess was Dinah,
she sprang a leak off China;
we had to pump poor Dinah's rump
to empty her vagina.

The cabin-boy's name was Nipper,
a dirty little flipper;
they filled his arse with broken glass
and circumcised the skipper.

The ladies of the nation
arose in indignation
and stuffed his bum with chewing-gum –
a smart retaliation!

The captain's wife was Mabel,
always willing and able,
behind the door, or on the floor,
or on the chart room table.

The captain had a daughter,
she fell into the water;
ecstatic squeals revealed that eels
had found her sexual quarter.

When we put into Calais,
the captain's daughter, Sally,
dressed as a whore she rushed ashore
and won the grand prix rally.

Another daughter, Charlotte,
she was a filthy harlot,
her thighs at night were lily-white,
but in the morning scarlet.

The ship's dog's name was Rover
the whole crew did him over;
they ground and ground that poor old hound
from Land's End round to Dover.

The ship's cat's name was Kitty;
her arse was black and shitty;
her feline twat was kept red-hot
by a crew who knew no pity.

So now we end this serial
from sheer lack of raw material;
we wish you luck, whenever you fuck,
from all disease venereal.

Anon

There was a young girl whose frigidity

There was a young girl whose frigidity
Approached cataleptic rigidity,
   Till you gave her a drink,
    When she quickly would sink
In a state of complaisant liquidity.

Anon

There was a young woman from Harlesden

There was a young woman from Harlesden
Who sucked off her man in the garden
   He said 'I want to know
    Where does my sperm go?'
She swallowed and said 'Beg your pardon?'

Anon

In the Garden of Eden lay Adam

In the Garden of Eden lay Adam
Complacently stroking his madam,
   And loud was his mirth
   For he knew that on earth
There were only two balls — and he had 'em.

Anon

INDEX OF FIRST LINES

A beautiful lass from Saigon   175
A buxom young fellow from London came down   234
According to old Sigmund Freud   52
A fair slim boy not made for this world's pain   4
A fellow with passions quite gingery   78
A gay boy who lived in Khartoum   79
A grave wise man that had a great rich lady   120
Ah! Cleft for me! the lover cries   83
All ye who know what pleasure 'tis to heave   103
A lonely young man from Norway   173
A modern young woman from France   127
Amyntas led me to a grove   39
Ancient person, for whom I   206
An old prostitute from Marseilles   213
An unfortunate pirate called Bates   175
A remarkable tribe are the Sweenies   174
A short-sighted sailor from Brighton   78
As I was walking down the town   51
A sweet disorder in the dress   3
A wanton young lady of Wimley   105
Away with silks, away with lawn   30
A weakling who lacked protoplasm   77
A woman waits for me, she contains all, nothing is lacking   89
A young violinist from Rio   22
Base metal hanger by your master's thigh!   138
Beneath the lamp the lady bowed   52
Be quiet, Sir! begone, I say!   19
Between your sheets you soundly sleep   96
Blessed above all other men is he   240
Blessed as the immortal Gods is he   50
Busts and bosoms have I known   151
But sweet-tooth Laura spoke in haste   64

Come, Madam, come, all rest my powers defy   33
Come, pretty nymph, fain would I know   146
Come rede me, dame, come tell me, dame   147
Come to me in my dreams, and then   182
Come to me in the silence of the night   188
Coming to kiss her lips such grace I found   29
Dainty darling, kind and free   44
Dildo has nose, but cannot smell   68
Doing, a filthy pleasure is, and short   40
Down in the land of King Farouk   222
Down lay the shepherd swain   115
Dreaming last night on Mrs Farley   101
Each man his humour hath, and, faith, 'tis mine   63
Earth to earth, sod to sod   220
Either she was foul, or her attire was bad   167
Fair Chloris in a pigsty lay   58
Faith, wench, I cannot court thy sprightly eyes   21
Gather ye rosebuds while ye may   213
Gellius is thin: why not? His mom   60
Gellius, why are your lips white as snow   65
'Given faith,' sighed the vicar of Deneham   104
Had we but world enough, and time   42
Hard by Pall Mall lives a wench called Nell   126
Have you beheld (with much delight)   139
Here lies the amorous Fanny Hicks   65
Here lies the body   172
He saw how at her length she lay   169
How happy were good English faces   164
I abhor the slimy kiss   61
I, being born a woman and distressed   165
I dreamed this mortal part of mine   166
If any man do want a house   142
If from the baths you hear a round of applause   137
I have a noble cockerel   136
i like my body when it is with your   88
I'll fuck you both right up the ass   239
In days of old when knights were bold   51
In hollow halls, with sparry roofs and cells   25
Innocent breasts, when I have looked upon them   179
In summer's heat and mid-time of the day   84

In the close covert of a grove   17
In the garden of Eden lay Adam   251
In winter, in my room   148
Ipsithilla, baby girl   92
I rise at eleven, I dine about two   119
It certainly is the smell of her cunt   94
I' th' isle of Britain, long since famous grown   109
It is not for the love of drink, that I   118
It was on the good ship *Venus*   245
I was fostered out to a woman called Fat Molly   199
I worship your fleece which is the perfect triangle   5
Lesbia, why are your amours   144
Let him kiss me with the kisses of his mouth   13
Long time he lay and hardly dared to breathe   72
Love a woman? You're an ass!   202
Love, I adore the contours of thy shape   201
Lying asleep between the strokes of night   91
Mad to be had, to be felt and smelled. My lips   31
may I feel said he   27
Methinks I see how the blessed swain was laid   16
Molly owned a shellfish stall   127
Much wine had passed, with grave discourse   121
My days of youth are over – my torch of life is out   211
My dearest, I shall grieve thee   7
My friend Billy's got a ten foot willy   151
My head is bald, my breath is bad   203
My Mall, I mark that when you mean to prove me   134
My mistress in a hive of bees   137
Naked I lay, clasped in my Callus' arms   35
Naked she lay, clasped in my longing arms   159
Nay, pish; nay, phew! nay, faith and will you? Fie!   117
None but a muse in love can tell   41
Now let me say good night; and so say you   98
No, worldling, no, 'tis not thy gold   204
Of like importance is the posture too   47
Oh! cunt is a kingdom, and prick is its lord   106
Once on a time the Sire of evil   150
O Rose, thou art sick!   161
O the parson is perverted in Mobile   235
Phyllis, when your old claws attempt to strum   207

Pull my arm back, Seymour 66
Romans, I appeal to you 111
Said old Lady H—, once a blooming young wench 221
She cried 'Laura,' up the garden 210
She lay all naked in her bed 157
Since thy third curing of the French infection 112
Sitting alone (as one forsook) 180
Sitting in O'Reilly's bar 226
St Agnes' Eve – Ah, bitter chill it was! 184
Stand, stately Tavie, out of the codpiece rise 150
Sylvia the fair, in the bloom of fifteen 20
Tell me, abandoned miscreant, prithee tell 218
That lovely spot which thou dost see 6
That time it was, as we in parlance wiled 75
The apprentice – fifteen, ugly, not too thin 110
The boy now fancies all the danger over 45
The hands explore tentatively 97
The last time I saw you, as like as two pins 57
The moth's kiss first! 181
The new cinematic emporium 77
The prick that once through Fanny's drawers 212
The proper way to eat a fig, in society 131
There is a thing which in the light 217
There once was a young man of Ghent 152
There was a young actress called Sue 173
There was a young couple called Kelly 79
There was a young fellow of King's 105
There was a young fellow of Lyme 76
There was a young girl whose frigidity 250
There was a young lady of Dover 104
There was a young man from Berlin 174
There was a young man of Devizes 152
There was a young plumber of Leigh 52
There was a young student of John's 76
There was a young woman from Harlesden 250
This is the female form 95
Those parts that attract male depravity 145
Though I be wooden Priapus (as thou seest) 140
To your question: why are my private parts 141
Tullia replies, my dear Octavia, you 56

Um Chukka Willy   135
Walking in a meadow green   162
Were Celia absent and remembrance brought   196
When a man grows old and his balls grow cold   228
When Francus comes to solace with his whore   60
When Love its utmost vigour does employ   86
When we were charming *Backfisch*   205
Who knows not now, my friend, the secret rites   93
Within a copse I met a shepherd-maid   15
With that he stripped him to the ivory skin   208
Would you be an angel   55
Years ago, at a private school   85
Young Corydon and Phyllis   48
Young Clovis by a happy chance   155
Your husband will be with us at the treat   113
You say I love not, 'cause I do not play   156

ACKNOWLEDGEMENTS

Thanks are due to the following copyright-holders for permission to reprint poems in this volume:

'An ever-fixed mark' by Kingsley Amis, from *A Look Round the Estate: Poems 1957–1967* by Kingsley Amis (Jonathan Cape), is reprinted by permission of Sir Kingsley Amis and Random House UK Ltd.

'The platonic blow' by W. H. Auden, from *The Faber Book of Blue Verse*, edited by John Whitworth, is reprinted by permission of the Estate of W. H. Auden and Faber and Faber Ltd.

'Late-flowering lust' by John Betjeman is reprinted by permission of John Murray (Publishers) Ltd.

Extract from *The Prologue to The Wife of Bath's Tale* by Geoffrey Chaucer, translated by David Wright, is reprinted by permission of the Peters Fraser & Dunlop Group Ltd.

'i like my body when it is with your' is reprinted from *Complete Poems 1904–1962* by E. E. Cummings, edited by George J. Firmage, by permission of W. W. Norton & Company Ltd. Copyright © 1925, 1976, 1991 by the Trustees for the E. E. Cummings Trust and George James Firmage.

'may i feel said he' is reprinted from *Complete Poems 1904–1962* by E. E. Cummings, edited by George J. Firmage, by permission of W. W. Norton & Company Ltd. Copyright © 1935, 1963, 1978, 1991 by the Trustees for the E. E. Cummings Trust and George James Firmage.